A Journey to Your Prophetic Destiny

Finding Fulfillment in God's Plan for Your Life

Prophet Stephen Fedele

Dedication

I would like to dedicate this book to Joanne Servello, first of all, for her love and commitment to the Lord Jesus Christ. I am grateful for her willingness and strength to never be ashamed of the message of the cross. I thank God and acknowledge the tremendous impact Joanne has had on my life. She continues to stand strong in His grace, lifting up and declaring, "To God be the glory!"

Acknowledgements

I want to take a moment to thank Dr. Wilson and his late wife, LouCelle, who took Rita and I under their wings and showed us all the ropes of traveling through Europe, mentoring us and helping us even further in the prophetic ministry that God called us to. Without their help and support, believing in us and investing in us, we would never have accomplished these last 25 years.

I also want to thank Marianne Lange and Jody Zilske for their help in bringing this book to completion.

Contents

Part 1

Destiny's Road

Part 2

The Fruit of Destiny

Preface

Life's paths often take us to places we didn't want to go with twists and turns that can leave us reeling. In those times, we need an anchor if we hope to navigate safely through the storms. This side of heaven no one escapes pain or suffering no matter how it may look to others, but with Jesus Christ as an anchor in those storms, there is always hope, direction and most importantly, purpose.

For me, looking back on my life one step, one connection at a time even in the worst and most discouraging circumstances, the hand of God could be found. Even before I was born, God was working. Psalm 139 tells us *He knew us from the womb*. With a longing in my heart even as a child, Christ was leading. As a poor, young boy from a broken family, picked on in school and in the neighborhood, I can look back and see God grooming and clearing the path to my destiny. There were those who spoke a word before I was born and those who prayed for me. Others God introduced into my life who carved paths and made a way for me, as well as those who came up alongside of me faithfully walking through both the darkness and the light. I am grateful for all of them and for a God who is always faithful. Within these pages, I want to show you that we all have a destiny, a God-given purpose for the kingdom. Be hopeful in Christ today no matter what today looks like for you. When you put your trust in Christ, He will lead you and show you the way, truly the best and most satisfying way for a life fulfilled in Him.

As you read this book, please keep pen and paper by your side and if the Lord impresses you with something, and you know He's talking directly to you, write it down. I believe there is a prophetic voice between the lines of this book. Be sensitive to how God may be speaking and believe there is a purpose for your life.

Foreword

Pastor Michael Servello Sr.

What a powerful book! As you read, you will get a glimpse into Steve's miraculous life journey. A journey filled with God's amazing grace, His unfathomable love, and the power of the gospel that changes and transforms lives!

I have known Steve just about my entire life. We were both from the same little upstate village of Herkimer, NY. We grew up in the same neighborhood and went to the same schools but yet we lived in two different worlds. Prior to our salvations, we were not friends. I had a wholesale produce business and Steve was one of my customers. When I would deliver vegetables to his pizzeria, I would send my girlfriend at the time (now my wife) to take his order while I waited in the truck. As a matter of fact, we often laugh as we remember how he would warn her, "Get away from that guy, he's no good for you!" He was certainly right as I was as lost in my darkness as Steve was in his; however, when Steve met Jesus, everything changed dramatically! His testimony will challenge you to believe no one is too far from God's love and power to save. This passage perfectly describes the power and wonder of salvation…

IICor.5:16-21…" This means that our knowledge of men can no longer be based on their outward lives (indeed, even though we knew Christ as a man we do not know him like that any longer). For if a man is in Christ he becomes a new person altogether—the past is finished and gone, everything has become fresh and new. All this is God's doing, for he has reconciled us to himself through Jesus Christ; and he has made us agents of the reconciliation. God was in Christ personally reconciling the world to himself—not counting their sins against them—and has commissioned us with the message of reconciliation. We are now Christ's ambassadors, as though God were appealing direct to you through us. As his personal representatives we say, "Make your peace with God." For God caused Christ, who himself knew nothing of sin, actually to be sin for our sakes, so that in Christ we might be made good with the goodness of God. *(J.B. Philipps)*

From the moment he was saved, Steve had an intense hunger for the Lord. He became a prayer warrior and began to join with my wife and mother in fervent prayer for my salvation. From the moment of my conversion, Steve became a huge part of my life. Praying for me, counseling me, often prophesying over me things that quickly came to pass which was an undeniable encouragement while we both learned to grow in our new found faith.

Soon after, Steve introduced us to a beautiful, talented and unbelievably funny girl named Rita, whom he married. She perfectly complemented Steve in every way! A match made in heaven. You cannot find more loyal friends in Christ than Steve and Rita. Our friendship and deep bond has lasted now for almost 50 years!

I have been Steve's friend, colleague but also his pastor. I have personally witnessed so many of the events Steve describes in the book. Steve's story is certainly not an American "pull yourself up by your bootstraps" message. This is a story only God Himself could write. A God story of someone abandoned and rejected by his earthly father, trying to fill that void looking for love and acceptance in all the wrong places. It depicts a journey that led him into deeper and deeper darkness that changed when he was introduced to his heavenly Father who offered him unconditional love, forgiveness and acceptance. Steve fully embraced Jesus and has never looked back!

This is a story about how God gives beauty for the ashes, creating something beautiful from what sin and life seemed to destroy. Steve was branded a failure and constantly told by those around him he would never amount to anything. Being pushed through school and graduated while being barely able to read, it seemed he was locked into a downward spiral of hopelessness. All that was changed when Steve met Jesus!

His devotion to Jesus, his love for people and his countless sacrifices laying down his life, again and again, is well known by those whom he has served. That young man, who few believed would amount to anything, was given a powerful call to ministry and a prophetic mantle that has blessed many and extended to the nations of the world. This book shares the hope we can have in God's purpose for each of us and His faithfulness to walk out that destiny with us as it becomes a reality.

International Foreword

Pastor Werner Lehmann,

I had been an elder for 10 years before becoming the first pastor in a church in Oron-la-Ville, Switzerland. In 1993, with my wife and a couple of friends, we traveled to Canada at the invitation of a pastor we knew. Our friend, Pierre Cyr introduced us to Steve and Rita Fedele which then led us to a ministerial meeting in Utica, New York.

The Fedeles prophesied over us through our translator, Diana, and we quickly realized the depth and the truthfulness of their ministry and also found out they wanted to serve Europe. When I came back to Switzerland, I talked about them to my elders' council. By joint agreement, we joyfully welcomed them and they came with a servant's attitude and great submission to the pastor and leaders.

In our discussions, the question of an apostolic and a prophetic covering came up. I was at the beginning of my full-time ministry after 10 years as an elder and a former farmer. The Fedeles taught us how important it is to have a spiritual covering and how to use it. This created a unanimous desire to step further into this process of welcoming Steve and Rita and a local ministry (Jean-Claude Chabloz) as a prophetic and apostolic covering. It was revolutionary for us and gave a strong empowerment to the future development of our small community located in a rural town of 1500 inhabitants. At this time, we were a hundred or so members and 20 years after, this church now counts more than 750.

The Fedeles were always reachable and willing to advise us and prayerful to seek the will of God. They were, of course, very appreciated by our church but also by other people. Indeed, during prophetic meetings, there was great participation. So many of their prophetic words helped people to achieve their call and identity as sons and daughters of God. We always have been astonished by how they gave true prophetic words and spoke into hundreds of people's lives in a single meeting—so extraordinary!

Speaking at least for myself as a pastor, Steve and Rita helped me to get into an apostolic ministry. They have also been a blessing through their prophetic voice and advice to my wife, Mado, and our children, particularly to my son Nicolas, who is today the senior pastor of this church.

I give thanks to God for all the time we have walked with Steve and Rita, for their love and resources and that they are still with us and our 8 churches (Gospel Center) that we have planted over these last years.

Steve and Rita - Thank you, we love you and we owe you so much.   Pastor Werner and Mado Lehman

Introduction

Destiny! Among words, this is one that conjures up all kinds of ideas. Ordinary, everyday people might feel destiny has nothing to do with them. That it's something for heroes or those known for doing unusual feats. You might say, "It's not about me." Wrong! We all have a destiny or purpose in life. In Jeremiah 29:11 God says, "For I know the plans that I have for you. They are for building up not tearing down for a future." In Psalm 139, God tells us that He covers us; He knew us in the womb. From our very earliest moments, God knew us. He created us for His glory and purpose. "Bring all who claim me as their God, for I have made them for my glory. It was I who created them." (Is. 43:7; NLT) For a moment let me reinforce those two things as this verse can be misused. It's for His glory and purpose. God has a perfect plan.

By sharing my story, I hope you will see how God's hand can be upon our lives in many ways. People and circumstances, which at times may seem random or chance occurrences, can be markers along our life's pathway. Horrible or challenging events can change our direction. Sometimes years might even pass before we become aware of the connections and how God in His mercy was always there.

The book begins with the early years of my life and the beginnings of the move of God in the Mohawk Valley. Besides my call, I examine some biblical examples of men and women who walked out their destinies despite challenging circumstances to find their purpose in God. Vital to the story is the growth of a small home meeting to the formation of a church that would evolve and become a force not only to affect the Valley but also to the nations of the world. The events of those early days demonstrate the importance of the local church in caring for people and developing ministry. It is from this local church, now known as Redeemer, that we were launched into our international ministries. We began to travel more until it became a full-time endeavor. God continued making connections and leading us in the way we should go. Today, we have reached twenty-five years of international travel and ministry. Praise the Lord!

Looking back over the years of my life, it seems staggering to consider all that God has done and how far He brought a poor boy from a disadvantaged family. More than anything else, I want to convey this thought: "For there is no respect of persons with God," or as the New Living Translation states, "God does not show favoritism." (Romans 2:11)

Most would not give a thought to the idea of a destiny or even a plan for our lives. We try to survive the day-to-day struggles that are inescapable. The best or most organized might say it's simply about having goals but our God is a God of detail. Scripture supports this; the very hairs of our head are numbered. (Mt. 10:30) Our names are engraved on the palms of His hand. (Is.49:16) He knows the down-sitting and uprising of our times. (Ps.139:2) We are not accidents. That's a common expression but don't be fooled. It plainly describes how well God knows us. A sparrow doesn't fall without His knowing. (Mt.10:29)

Often, we are so busy that we can walk through life not making connections, but I am going to challenge you to think about some of the key people and circumstances in your life as you read through my story. It takes time for destiny to unfold. There are numerous examples of those who waited years to see the Word of the Lord come to pass. That doesn't mean for years nothing happened or that everything that happened was bad. Think of Abraham; think of Joseph; think of David or Esther. They had trials but they also had successes along the way, accomplished things and moved forward. Above all, they understood the importance of seeking God and the privilege of hearing from Him. Don't forget that. Those concepts marked their lives and made a difference. I challenge you today—pray and believe God to direct your path. If He can do it for me, He can do it for you.

Over the last several years, the Lord has impressed upon me to tell my story. The problem was where do I begin? I came up with an original idea—start at the beginning! I was born July 6, 1951, in Utica, New York, about an hour from Albany, NY, the state's capital. My father was Frank James Fedele and my mother Domenico (Minnie) Nardelli. In the 1920's Utica, at one point, became famous as a stopover between New York City and Rochester for many of the mafia. It was even referred to in some of the old gangster stories as Sin City.

From 1977-1990, Utica was the place where I began my ministry as a pastor at The Full Gospel Church of Utica. Later, we changed the name to Solid Rock Church. But my destiny began long before that, and I believe this is true for all of us. As you continue to read this book, it will become clear to all that the plan God has for us is an eternal one. Again remember, Jeremiah. God had plans for him (Jer. 29:11) and even before that (Jer. 1:5) we see how far back God's purpose goes. The Word tells us that He knew us before He formed us in the womb. (Psalm 139) It goes on to say that "before you were born I set you apart." Think about that. Before we were even born, God knew us and set us apart for a purpose.

Part One: Destiny's Road

Chapter 1

Even From the Womb

Perhaps you're not convinced of the idea of destiny or that there are connections, or maybe a pathway divinely planted for us to choose. I would like to share a testimony with you that may give you something more to think about.

It was 1951. A family was going through very hard times when the mother became pregnant. The father didn't want any more children. At the time, the only children in the family were girls. The family name, it seemed, would not be carried on; a most important Italian value appeared to be slipping away.

The man took his wife to an abortion mill where his mother held his wife's hands back while the abortion was performed with a coat hanger. With this great trauma, the wife was so overcome with grief, she suffered from mental illness (schizophrenia) for many years from that point on and was plagued with delusions, fear and torment.

It wasn't long after the abortion that the woman seemed to continue to feel life in her womb. She went to her mother's home and remained there. Sure enough, she gave birth to a baby boy. Of course, that was cause for a great celebration. The families came back together and the baby boy received the name of his grandfather.

In 1948, three years before the abortion and the birth of the baby boy, there is another story. The grandfather was a very cruel man and part of the mafia. He was what they called the Black Hand. His job was to go to storekeepers and collect a portion of money and bring it to the godfather. There was one store that he went to where he would be especially cruel to the man. They were the Mancusos. He would slap him around in front of his wife and children. The reason he hated that storekeeper so much was because he was a spirit-filled Christian Pentecostal. In fact, the Pentecostal church was only three doors down from this family's house.

The storekeeper's wife was a praying woman. One day when the mafia grandfather came into the store and raised his hand to the woman's husband, the woman, Mrs. Mancuso, stopped the man's hand and didn't fear what that could've meant for the business or her family. She knew she had a message from God for this man. She put her finger in the face of the mafia man and pointed directly at him saying these words, "The child that receives your name will preach the gospel of my God." Mrs. Mancuso walked away only to turn and come back to him with her finger once again in his face and said, "…and he will preach the gospel of my God to the nations of the world."

Did I not tell you or did you already guess the man's name? Yes, his name was Stefano Fedele, my grandfather, and I was that baby—the baby, who if the natural course of events had fully played out, would have been aborted.

I know you'll have questions, so let me try to answer them. First of all and most importantly, if everyone has a destiny and there are no mistakes, then what happened to the destiny of my twin? I don't want to seem super spiritual but the Word of God says there are instances where we must stand in the gap for those who cannot stand for themselves. I know there are times where I'm holding up more than just my destiny. (Ez. 22:30) This is true for all of us, for the countless thousands of lives that have been destroyed. They each had a purpose and that's why we must do all we can, not only for ourselves but for them and others for God's glory.

Another question might be how could you possibly know about the abortion especially since your mother was schizophrenic? When my mother got sick, she would cry and say to me, "They got the other baby but they didn't get you." By the grace of God, two years before my mother died, the Lord healed her and she told me the story of the abortion.

How could I possibly know about what the woman said to my grandfather? I knew because Mrs. Mancuso said it to my face. Years later when I opened my new business, I appeared on the local news. During the grand opening, I dedicated the business to the Lord. After seeing the news on TV, Mrs. Mancuso came to church and I heard of the incident directly from her! How faithful God is to reveal the path! It may not happen at the time you expect, but He is always leading.

Know this, every connection can count. God is always with us and knew that you would be reading this book. God wants you to know that you have a destiny as well. Even from the womb.

Chapter 2

My Early Life

For years, I never really gave much thought about the very beginning of my life. I knew early on my parents' marriage was broken. Seeing my father grabbing my mother and throwing hot, boiling water on her, traumatized me as well as my sister, Pat. My childhood was unhappy and painful. It consisted of feeling shame and being bullied. I was very afraid of the future. Is this all there would be? It seemed, certainly, there was nothing to look forward to.

I had suffered emotional and physical abuse from a very early age from people outside my immediate family. This was something I kept hidden because if my grandmother (my mother's mother) ever knew, heads would have rolled. At the cross of Jesus, I was able to forgive and release them. I also realized that I had become an enabler allowing them access to my life, but by the power of the blood of Jesus, I could break that vicious cycle.

Being brought up by my mother, I became an easy target. She did everything she possibly could for us including sneaking out very late in the evening to wash dishes and clean a restaurant just to have some extra money. We were on public assistance so she had to do it quietly not drawing any attention. From the abuse and distress, she suffered from multiple emotional problems and was a schizophrenic. Sometimes, all I knew was, today, mom was happy.

9

Then for months, she would be out of it. As early as I can remember, I became responsible for her care. By the grace of God and with the help of my wife, Rita, she remained with us until she went home to the Lord. I thank God for that wonderful privilege of leading her to the Lord and caring for her.

The one bright spot in my youth was my mother's mother, Pasqualina Genny Nardelli. I lived to please her and I idolized her; she was everything to me and I loved her very much. Because of my mother's family and especially my Aunt Ella, who was also like a mother to me, I've often thought I had three mothers. I loved Ella and was devoted to her. I had promised my grandmother I would always be there for Ella. She never had any children and became a widow at the early age of thirty-six.

Despite the hard times, I also have some wonderful memories. Every Sunday morning the entire family would meet at my grandmother's house for coffee and fried dough with powdered sugar. It was my favorite time then and still is now as it has become a tradition that I share with my grandchildren. When I'm home, I'll try to make it every Sunday for them. As a young child, another fond memory was Christmas Eve which was a very special time when the whole family would be together at my grandmother's. These traditions were probably the highlight of my life during those difficult days.

My grandmother and I had a close relationship; she used to say to me, "Don't you ever bring mud into my house." I knew she was saying don't ever bring any shame or disgrace to our home. I used to joke and say that the soles of my shoes were the cleanest but truly my soul was very dark and sinful. Despite what I thought or how I felt, I never let a day go by that I did not see my grandmother. As I got older, I was always doing something for her. It was a great joy for me. My nickname for her was Don Gen. She was dear to my heart.

During the summer of 1973 on a hot August day, I took a break from work and went to my grandmother's house. As I approached her house, I saw about 100 people across the street outside the Youth Center for the Pentecostal church. When I got closer, I realized that they were praying and knew that would greatly upset my grandmother. This may not be everyone's experience but it was for me with my strong Italian background. My grandmother would begin some retaliatory action. I am referring to something called the Malocchio or evil eye, where some believe you could put curses on people. Additionally, you could also have the ability to break the curse. At that time, I believed that my grandmother had both abilities. It followed naturally, that she and I proceeded to throw curses on them by putting a red ribbon on her dog Ginger and herself. We walked back-and-forth in front of her windows just saying ridiculous things, such as, "May you itch for several years, that your dinner will burn or you get a flat tire." Of course, nothing happened but it made us feel better. My grandmother was a character, but I loved her dearly.

Later when I began to read the Bible, I thought my life was like Timothy's. He was being brought up by his grandmother and his mother. His father was absent. Some accounts state that Timothy might have had a fearful spirit (1 Cor.16:10) and another verse (1 Tim. 5:23) suggests he often had stomach infirmities. He was sickly, shy, timid, not the most likely to succeed and even more likely to be passed over. But for God!

As for me, I was an awkward and even backward person. I gave everybody a lot of material to use against me. I remember my teachers talking about me saying I was the stupidest kid they had ever known. Don't feel bad for me; they were telling the truth. I used to joke a lot and say that it took me three years longer to get out of school than anyone else because I loved it so much.

The truth is I did it for grandmother. She insisted I finish school since she never had that opportunity. She was married at the age of thirteen and a mother by fourteen. Her choice was either get married or be put in an orphanage because of a family tragedy that had taken place. She used to say that I had murder in my blood and nobody better cross me. Her father, my great grandfather, had killed someone. She loved him so much and told the story of the tragic event when he died in the Jamesville prison in New York State. My grandmother went door to door raising money to bring him home to bury him. I have a sheet of paper with all those who donated. One of the first to give was James Servello. His son, Sam Servello, the owner of the Herkimer Chief grocery store, along with his

12

daughter-in-law Joanne Servello, and his daughter Angie were among the first who began to intercede and pray for me to come to Christ in the years ahead. His grandson, Michael Servello, became my best friend and as we were saved, we began to walk in the things of God together. We had no idea then of the great plans God had in store for us. We just knew we loved Jesus and wanted to share Him with others. This friendship grew and so did our understanding of the plans the Lord had for the Mohawk Valley, but as kids, we had little understanding of all these things. We had no idea what we were stepping into at that time. Looking back now, we can see the divine hand of God in every step even the difficult ones. For me, as a child, there were still many painful years to come.

I was the kind of person who loved to get people to laugh with me. That way, they were not laughing at me. I probably have what would be called a learning disability. I was unable to read for all my school years. I had many tutors who tried to help but there was just some mental block, and I could not do it.

As you can imagine, my school life was not happy, although I found a spot of hope in the drama club. They gave me an opportunity to pretend to be someone else. There I had some friends and I enjoyed it very much. Usually, I would get a standing ovation for my one line in the play. What was amazing is that my fear of speaking in front of people seemed to vanish. A couple of years before that in an English class, we had to give a speech about our life. I remember standing in front of my classmates that day and all I could say was, "My name is Steve Fedele." I repeated it several times. Finally, one of my classmates said, "Shut up, stupid, and sit down. We know your name."

Some would say what's in a name anyway? But I believe that day when I announced my name was Stephen Fedele held a key that would unlock my destiny. Sometimes when I'm preaching, I'll say, "How many of you have your first name in the Bible?" Of course, there would be several people. I would then ask, "How many of you have your last name in the Bible?" There might be one or two. Occasionally, I would say, "How many of you have your first and last name in the same verse?" There were never any who would have this unique characteristic. But I would say, "I do!" In Acts 6:5 it states that "Stephen was faithful." My last name, Fedele, means faithful.

When I was thirteen years old, it was in that same year that other things began to align and bring me into my destiny. I had absolutely no idea what was taking place in the spiritual realm. Usually, most of us would not, but God knows and orchestrates the good, the bad, and the ugly in our lives to bring us to our destiny.

One day, I'd been out playing with some friends in an abandoned building and I stepped on a rusty nail. I was too afraid to tell my mother so I just soaked it in a dirty mop pail. My leg got so big it was about four times the size it should have been! I became very ill and whether a dream or vision, I remember I was sinking deeper and deeper towards what seemed like a very bright marble floor. I was just hovering over this floor when I sensed something; it wasn't a voice but a thought that came to me and said, "It's not your time yet."

I never really talked about this for many years because my father would tell a similar story that happened to him in December 1951, when I was just six months old. He was working in a laundromat in Utica, New York called Liberty Laundry. At 12 noon, he was the only employee in the building when it exploded. He was burned from the top of his head to the soles of his feet and pronounced dead at Saint Elizabeth's Hospital in Utica, New York. He related an experience he had at the time. My father said that he was hovering over his body and the doctors and nurses were there. He felt like he sent the message that there was money in his pocket and the doctor said to the nurse, "Check his pockets." As she went to check his pockets, he was back in his body. He never considered it a religious experience, except occasionally he would say that the man up there didn't want him yet. I never wanted to be anything like him, and so I would never tell the story of what happened to me but I can surely tell you, I thought about these similar occurrences.

After I heard that voice and message, the next thing I knew, I woke up and found my grandmother and several of the older ladies of my neighborhood sitting around already in black preparing for my final breath. They had put salt pork on my foot which drew the poison out and spared my life. It's a memory that was so instilled in me because of my grandmother. She had lost two sons, one at a very early age, thirteen just like me. My Uncle Vincent had cut the palm of his hand slicing some bread and was afraid to tell her. He hid it from her and got lockjaw and died. She used to cry often for her son. At that time, the Catholic Church would not allow his body in the church for a funeral for fear what he died from was contagious. To make matters worse, my grandmother didn't have a new bed sheet to put on his bed. That would be a significant part of laying someone out in the home. When I woke up from my experience, the one thing I noticed immediately was all the bedding was brand-new.

Years later when my aunt passed away and I inherited my grandmother's house from her, I was cleaning it out. I found two trunks. I always wondered what was in those trunks, what kind of treasures I would find. I never had the courage to look in them over the years, but now they were mine. When I opened them, I was shocked at what I found. Inside lay a newspaper article about her father (my great-grandfather) and a murder but that was not all. Hundreds of white flat sheets! My grandmother used to say no one will ever die without a clean sheet! Not knowing what else to do, I gave all those sheets to a mission in Africa.

Life continued to be difficult on every front. School was especially hard. I had no insight or understanding of what was happening during those years. I've joked and said that I wrote a book when I was in high school which was *36 Different Ways to Get Home* because it always seemed like there was some bully ready to beat me up. My older sister, Ange, would go after the bullies for me. On the day she was going to be married while coming home from the beauty shop with her wedding veil in her hand, she got after a couple of them and came to my rescue. The bullies got the last laugh in the end because my sister soon moved away and I was on my own again.

That story was important because of the events that followed. A new kid came to school. His name was Gregory, and he was mentally challenged. If that wasn't enough for the bullies, he was a Pentecostal. Where I lived in a small upstate New York town, a church like that was a target for ridicule. His coming from this background is what I think intrigued me most about Gregory. He was always talking about the Lord. At the same time this was happening, I was searching for God. I had gone to almost every church from the Jehovah Witnesses, the Mormons, even to a Jewish temple, but I did not go to the Pentecostal church. People called it the devil's church.

The nuns at the Catholic school and I had a shaky relationship. At one point, they asked me to leave the school because I confronted them on the fact that they gave a passing grade to another student because her parents were a wealthy family. One day, just to agitate them, I rang the doorbell and as they came to the door they said, "Stephen, we don't want trouble!" The Pentecostal church was directly across from the main door of the convent. I walked

17

slowly across the street to the front door of what they called the devil's church. I waved to them and opened the door knowing how this would shock and upset them. I was curious about this church but I didn't dare go all the way inside. I was very Roman Catholic. My grandmother and I would attend novenas and masses almost daily but I had fun that day shaking up the nuns.

I only knew one person who went to that church. She was my neighbor at one time, a little Italian lady, and my grandmother told me to be respectful because she belonged to one of the more prominent families in our village. We called her Aunt Zianest. My grandmother also warned me never to listen to her about her church. I remember when I was about eight years old, her house and mine were between two other houses and you had to walk up a long driveway to get to these homes. A murder had taken place there which and had been attributed to my great-grandfather. On Sunday mornings, when this woman was returning from church, that driveway seemed to light up and she would come over to me. Usually, I would be sitting on my steps, maybe even waiting for her to come. She would put her hand on my heart and say to me, "Stefano, you need Jesus" and she would pray over me.

One evening around that same time period, I was playing with some friends near the Pentecostal church. Inside, they were singing "There is Power in the Blood." That night, I threw a rotten tomato through the window and hit an older lady. I remember her face and her hair was in a holiness bun. She looked directly out the window at me. It was so dark she couldn't have seen who I was, but she said, "Lord, get that one!" I ran home and slept under my bed that night. I believe God answered her prayer. Thank you, Jesus!

I didn't understand at that moment of time but my destiny was beginning to open before me. Gregory, the new boy in the neighborhood, gave me a nickname—Pope Fedele! He would say to me, "Pope Fedele! These boys are threatening my life and my mom doesn't have money for a funeral. We just buried granddad." To this day, some of my closest friends, in fun, will refer to me as Pope Fedele.

At that point, I took it upon myself to bring Gregory home each day to protect him, which was funny. I couldn't even protect myself, but I felt compelled to do it for him. Gregory and his mom lived in a small area of the Pentecostal church parsonage. When I brought him home and knocked on the front door of the parsonage, it was the Pastor, Dr. Eldon Wilson, who opened the door and invited me inside. Little did I know that twenty years later he would be the one who would open the doors to Europe and ignite our international ministry. As a boy at that first meeting, I had no idea of the importance of the connection I had just made.

From that time forward over several months, Dr. Wilson's wife, LouCelle, and Gregory's mother began to share the love of Jesus with me but because of my upbringing, I would make fun of them and call them names. One day when I arrived at school, I saw the student body all around the little red fire alarm box that was on

19

the front lawn. As I made my way over to see what was going on, there was Gregory. All the kids were taunting him to open that little glass door and put a quarter in and pull the lever. They were telling him he was going to hear his favorite song, *The Old Rugged Cross.* I don't know where I got the courage, but I stepped through the crowd of students and said, "Come with me! Gregory, don't do it!" and I brought him to class. Of course, that did not make me very popular.

Things continued to get worse for me. The coach of the high school decided that at noon the next day I would wrestle the school's champion wrestler. I remember walking to school that morning with two sisters who lived near me. They said, "Steve don't go! Go home! Don't go!" Truthfully, I was thinking the same thing. My thoughts were, *You better turn and run.* I want to tell you that's exactly what I wanted to do—run! But I heard a voice and it said, *If you turn and run today, you will have to run the rest of your life.*

Scripture tells us, "I have not given you a spirit of fear and timidity, but of power, love, and self-discipline." (2 Tim. 1:7) I did not know the Lord, but I believe it was the Spirit speaking to me because I was going to need strength for the destiny He had called me to. I would have to conquer my fears, limitations and insecurities. There would be times where I would have to face demonic spirits. We all have our fears and must learn how to face them or they will rule us.

20

Thank God for His grace and Word. We need to constantly remind ourselves, *we were not given a spirit of fear.* At that young age, I was beginning to face fear not realizing how important it would be for my future.

Physically, I was very skinny. If a strong wind came along, I could be blown away. The gymnasium had a balcony. Once again, several hundred students came to watch. The potential was there that I would be slaughtered but just the opposite happened. Something changed in me and I began to realize I didn't have to be a victim. I had a choice just like the choice I made to face that wrestling champion. It may be hard to believe but I don't really remember the outcome that day. I like to think I won. People began to look at me differently even some of the most popular athletes and girls in the school began to be friendlier and kinder to me. Something was happening!

A Defining Moment

On that same day I took Gregory home, I remember it was bright and sunny. As we approached the parsonage, I saw a group of people standing outside greeting one another with great joy. Little did I know that another dimension of my destiny and unlocking of the future God had for me was underway. I was totally unaware. Perhaps it can be likened to Moses standing at the Red Sea with his enemies behind him and the Red Sea before him. He knew he could not turn back and yet he did not feel able to go forward. But the Lord was at work from the other side of the Red Sea with a mighty

21

wind making a way. We serve a God who makes a way when there seems to be no way.

The group of people standing outside the little Pentecostal church that day when I took Gregory home were the very people who became instrumental and supported me years later. Pastor Wilson was the one who introduced me to each of them who would eventually play very important roles in my life and years later bring about God's word and destiny. During those early days with Pastor Wilson in that little church, I met Pastor Mickey Mingo and his wife, Deanna, Sister Gloria Wine and Eleanor Webb from the West Coast and years later through them, I met Pastor Bill Hamon, who is still a renowned prophet and teacher today. Eventually, I also met Pastor Reg Layzell, a great man of God and father of the 1948 revival. When I first met these great men and women of God, I had no idea the extent and privilege of their influence or what God had for me at that time. Certainly as a young boy, I could not have imagined that God was at work.

In the years to come, Mickey Mingo became our pastor and if it wasn't for him, we would never have been released into the ministry. Everyone would've passed us by but by the grace of God, Mickey saw something in us. Once again what can I say but thank you, Jesus! Sister Gloria Wine was the pastor of Mickey Mingo, Eldon Wilson, and Bill Hamon. These were and are great men of God used throughout the country. Pastor Mingo went on to be with the Lord but was a key influence in starting multiple churches in upstate New York. Doctor Eldon Wilson and Pastor Bill Hamon are still ministering today and are mighty men of God. Sister Wine became one of our greatest mentors. We spent many hours together at our home and in church as she ministered and shared her experience and helped us grow in Christ.

A few days before she passed, on her deathbed Sister Wine called us and said, "I have everything settled in my life but two things. First Rita, I release my prophetic and pastoral mantle to you and secondly, I ask a favor. I want to make sure Eleanor Webb is taken care of." Eleanor Webb was her traveling companion and had been a missionary for many years in Uganda, Africa when Idi Amin was killing and persecuting Christians. Eleanor has a powerful testimony of how God protected her in those days. She had no family to speak of and Sister Wine asked if Eleanor could live with us. She came to us and what a blessing it was! Eleanor lived with us for many years and was our church secretary, prayer warrior, Bible teacher, friend and like a grandmother to our children. We will be forever grateful for all she did for us during those years. She made our ministry possible. We thank you, Eleanor, for that. Then Bill Hamon, one of the world's premier prophets, became the first to lay hands on us and pronounce the prophetic ministry. Fifteen years later, he pronounced the apostolic call upon us. He visited our church many times and left a great impartation.

Perhaps the greatest treasure was Pastor Reg Layzell, the father of the 1948 revival, whom we did not meet early on, but because

23

of my relationship with the pastors I've mentioned, a blessed connection was made. What a privilege and an honor to serve him! He passed away while he was in Utica, New York. Many people were clamoring for his mantle. This is something I've never mentioned before but I know that his mantle fell upon my friend, Michael Servello. The apostolic pastoral heart went to him and the world mission, prophetic anointing fell upon me.

While in Utica, Pastor Reg Layzell fell into a coma and his children came from different parts of the world to be with him. We hosted them at our home for several weeks until their dad passed. He was hospitalized in Saint Elizabeth's Hospital in Utica, New York, and several days after he went into the hospital, the head of the staff came to me and asked, "Who is this man? We're getting calls from around the world and we had to put more operators on the phone lines." I was able to share a little of the great man of God that he was and all that God was able to do throughout his life.

I remember one Sunday morning on my way to church I said to Rita, "I'm just going to stop at the hospital to make sure the family has everything they need." When I walked into the room, his daughter, Marion Peterson, said, "Dad, look. It's Pastor Fedele!" He raised that one eyebrow and commented, "Bless God! He might make a preacher someday."

In that short time when he came out of his coma, he declared something so powerful it has always stayed with me, and I've declared it many times. It was "Occupy until He comes." Luke 19:13

tells the story of the man of noble birth who gave finances to his slaves and said, "Put this to work until I come back." Essentially, it means to carry on the family business. What he was declaring was, "Continue to preach the gospel of Jesus Christ." By the grace of God, that's what my wife, Rita, and I desire to do, and we believe our children and grandchildren will also carry on the family business.

The most important thing I can convey is that even as a child before I knew the Lord personally, He was laying the groundwork for my life. So long ago in challenging circumstances, God was putting people in my path who would have a profound effect upon my ministry many years in the future. God always has a purpose for us. As we seek Him, His light will shine upon our paths and make the crooked places straight.

Chapter 3

What I Planned and What God Did

On the day I finally graduated from high school, I was on the platform to receive my diploma and the principal, Mr. Garbler, said, "Perhaps you will open your own pizzeria, and we'll all come!" Everybody applauded and laughed. Of course, my grandmother was there sitting so proudly and when she heard that, something went off in her heart and mind and she thought, *Yes, he needs to have his own place!* If you can picture her, she was very strong, determined, and bold. I had worked ever since I was 10 years old. My grandmother had taken it upon herself to go into the restaurant where I was working and said to the owners, Paul and Yolanda Yetty, "My Stephen has worked here faithfully for nine years opening and closing, making all the purchases, hiring and firing workers basically running the restaurant as his own." She went on, "You know you don't have any children and my Stevie has been here working, faithfully. Give him a cut of the business, make him a partner." Paul said, "No!"

Yolanda and I were very close. She was a lovely, godly woman and very hard-working. She really pleaded with me not to leave. The burden of the business was primarily on her shoulders, but I began to think about it. I realized I had to do something for myself

27

and provide security for my mother or I would spend my whole life there. That was it! I decided I would open my own place. Because I really cared about the Yettys, I opened my pizzeria two villages away and made my pizza a different style not to be in competition with them. The restaurant became an overnight success. My grandmother made my first batch of meatballs and the entire family came to help the weekend of my grand opening. In so many ways, my family, especially my Uncle John Licari and my mother, were always there for me. I called my restaurant Stefano's Pizzeria; it was in Ilion, New York.

At that point, my life was still on the dark side. I had been doing the same job for so long everything was just on the automatic pilot. The restaurant had opened in October of 1972. As a restaurateur, I worked around the clock, 70 plus hours a week. This was about the same amount of time I had worked at Yettys, but that was my life. I enjoyed working with the public and meeting people and having money to do whatever I wanted to do. Now that I had the money, there was no time to spend it. I was clearing $1800 a week for myself after I paid all my expenses. Somehow, I still didn't feel satisfied.

One day my good friend, Fran, and I decided that we were going to go to a food show at a nearby community college. We set off for the day looking to see the new equipment and other items that might be out on the market. We walked around and sampled some food and looked at the equipment that was on display. Fran had also worked in the pizza business for years so we spent most of the day there. In the late afternoon, I went by a booth and saw a young lady and started talking to her. We talked for a brief time. When I walked away, I said to my friend, "See the girl over there? I'm going to marry her." Fran said to me; "What's her name?" I said, "I don't know." We never exchanged names. I didn't think about it for a long time. Once again, my destiny was unfolding before my eyes, but I had no idea. Yes, it was Rita. That was fall 1972.

In the providence of God, in September of 1972, Rita accepted a teaching job in Herkimer, New York, my hometown. She had an aid who happened to be a friend of mine from high school, Julie Decarr. One night, Julie said to Rita that a friend of hers had opened a pizza shop. She suggested going and having something to eat. They walked into my restaurant and Rita called out, "The Kentucky Fried Chicken guy!" She insisted that earlier that week we had met at a Kentucky Fried Chicken and that I had tried to pick her up. Rita and I connected immediately. We enjoyed being with one another and shared a lot of laughter and joy. For the next several months, we dated. I met her family, and she met mine. At first, my grand-mother thought that Rita was a long-lost relative I had found for her. On Rita's side, her parents were impressed by me. I had my own business and her father also had his own business. He was a barber for many years and respected by many. He worked hard and thought it would be great for his daughter and me to get together.

Early in our dating, Rita decided she would help my mother get her driver's license. My mother had to rely on me totally for all her transportation. At that point, Rita still didn't know the full impact of my mother's mental state. Without me knowing, as she wanted to surprise me, she decided to take my mother to get her permit. Rita had no hint that might not be a good idea. Happily, she told me that she took Minnie for her permit and that my mother passed with flying colors! What started off as a seemingly helpful and positive idea quickly ended. Thank God that Rita took her for her first driving lesson in an abandoned parking lot. Behind the wheel, my mother had a panic attack. Her legs stiffened and were pressing on the gas. Rita had to spring into action and take over as they had missed hitting the brick wall of the abandoned building by inches. That was my mother's first and last lesson. This was important to me as I felt that I had to explain to Rita the tragic story of my mother's life and why she was in such a mental state. From that point on, Rita was always so supportive and helpful both to me and my mother. She showed the same love for my mother as I did. This meant so much to know that I could count on her to understand I would never be able to put my mother in a nursing home and that we would have to make a place for her in our home.

Rita was a teacher and a fabulous cook. If you ever ate at our home, you would know that. We were going to open a catering business, expanding the restaurant. The plan was to build our own home. I promised her that every August we would close the restaurant and travel the world. The first place she wanted to go was Spain. We had it all planned. Also, we both were Roman Catholic so that was the cherry on top. If you know anything about Italian culture, you know that sums it up. Our path seemed clear. But as we began to get more serious and talk marriage, even to the point of getting engaged, I said to Rita, "I can't marry you. I love you too much. If I marry you, I will destroy your life." I knew in my heart that I loved her very much, but I also knew there still that dark side of me—a lot of fear and bondage from my youth. Things between us seemed unsettled and at the end of the school year, Rita resigned from her teaching position to do her Master's degree. At the time, she lived outside of Albany, New York, about an hour and a half from Herkimer. That move marked the end of our relationship or so we thought. We remained good friends and would see one another occasionally. One time she brought a new boyfriend into the restaurant and I made my waitress spill the pasta on his lap— oops! There was a part of me that was sad because I knew in my heart Rita was the one for me. When my grandmother and my family would say, "Where's Rita?" I would say, "She's gone home to finish her degree." For the time, it seemed our plans were not to be.

I remember that was late August. This was about the time the Servellos had a terrible crisis with their daughter, Judy. It was a dramatic crisis that affected the lives of many, including me and led to my salvation. As you read in *Joanne's Story*, her daughter, a beautiful, healthy 17-year-old girl, suddenly began to act

31

strangely. The family didn't know what to do so they brought her to the doctor. One thing led to another and she ended up in a mental institution weighing less than that 90 pounds. It was a horrible experience to walk through but one that changed the Servellos' lives forever, and not only theirs but on a greater scale the climate of the Mohawk Valley as well.

Chapter 4

Joanne's Story

Joanne Servello, known to many as Mama Servello, is one of the key individuals bringing Jesus and the movement of the Holy Spirit to the Mohawk Valley. I know the influence she had on my life and the lives of many of my contemporaries. This is her story of the miracle that occurred in her life and family that touched so many and opened the door to Christ for countless numbers of people. This miracle touched my life and was one of the key events that firmed my foothold on the path of destiny. Today, she still shares the Good News and the power of the gospel. Joanne, I am forever grateful.

Joanne's Story: The Power of God at Work

For many years I wanted to write the story, but you know they say time heals everything. I was working as a receptionist at the church that my son, Michael Servello, and Steve Fedele started years earlier that came as a direct result of this testimony. My grandson now is the Pastor and one day he brought a young man to me who was about to become a new member of our church. I was so amazed by what the young man said. He began to relate how he worked in the state mental hospital a few years ago. "I've heard all about your daughter, Judy, and the story of what happened to her there." He then began to tell me word for word what occurred so

33

many years ago. I knew the Lord had sent him to remind me of the wonderful miracle He had worked in our lives and continues to use even today.

It has been over 40 years since the Lord Jesus Christ came into my life in such a powerful way. Not only was I converted, but many others came to know the Lord. Steve Fedele was one of my first converts. It all began when my beautiful 17 year-old daughter, Judy, came home one night and said, "Mommy, I'm dying." I took her hand and could feel her spirit leaving her body. She began talking as if she was out of her mind. The next day, her father and I took her to the doctor. That was the beginning of our nightmare that seemed as if it would never end...but for God.

I began to think about those dark days of my life. I could smell again the foul odor of the mental hospital. I could see the mile-long ugly, dark hallways and hear the keys turning and the doors slamming. It was like being caught in the middle of a nightmare. At the time, I was approaching middle-age. I felt empty. My children were in their teens. I was a hairdresser and my husband had a produce company. It seemed to others that our family had everything. We had a beautiful home, many friends and were seemingly religious. We didn't go to church much, but we were brought up to believe that there was a good Lord.

My lifestyle did not leave much room for God. The discontent was so great, and I felt so empty. About the same time, I had some Christians who would come into my beauty shop and as I was doing their hair, they would share with me about the love of God. One of them gave me a New Testament which had the sinner's prayer. I said it that day and I signed my name at that moment under the prayer. Little did I know that simple step would be the beginning of the Lord Jesus Christ showing me His mercy and love which continues with me to this day. He was about to take everything good and bad in my life and bring me to my destiny. Thank you, Jesus, for your love.

That night when my daughter said she was dying began the darkest months of my life. She grew worse every day. We brought her to the local hospital. The doctors and the staff had no idea what to do for her. I would sit by her bed for hours and no one would come in to even see or check on her. I was so afraid to leave her. The doctor, by all reports, who was supposed to be this brilliant physician, said to me, "I cannot help her. All she wants to talk about are dead bodies." Endlessly, they told me they had no answers and could no longer help her.

From there she was sent to a mental institution. I knew deep in my heart that there was no help for my daughter by any human resource or agent. I had to totally depend on my God. Her condition was spiritual and I believe the Lord began to show me that demons were bringing her into a dark cave. Her screams were heartbreaking, "Please don't let me go there again! Help me!" I was so troubled because I knew there was no help from the doctors. I had to resolve in my heart that I would have to seek every answer from God, and I would have to expect a miracle from heaven for Judy.

I sought out one of the young physicians on the ward and told him my daughter had demons and his reply was, "You know, I do not have time to treat you right now. I only have time to help your daughter." As he looked at her, while she was propped up in a high-chair with restraints, he said, "What a shame that someone so beautiful would end up like this." At that moment, Judy had to use the bathroom so, with some of the orderlies, we got her up. On the wall in the bathroom was a mirror. She looked in the mirror and said, "I'm so ugly!" I said to the doctor, "She is so beautiful; why would she say that?" He said, "That's how she sees herself."

A few days later, I arrived at the hospital and I saw my daughter walking with the help of the orderlies. She was making weird gestures as she was walking and looked at me with a blank stare not really knowing me. I said, "Judy!" because she could not recognize me. With a mocking unrecognizable voice that was not Judy, the spirit in her said, "Like mother, like daughter!" I remember thinking, *How wicked I must be that all this has come upon my daughter*! The condemnation was so great I felt like someone had literally punched me in the stomach.

The pain, the anguish and the fear that were consuming my heart were impossible to bear. I could not even begin to put it into words realizing it was such a hopeless situation through natural eyes. But my cry to God was heard that evening.

At home, the doorbell rang and when I answered it, there were two gentlemen standing before me. They introduced themselves; one was Pastor Nick Welch and the other was one of his elders, Jerry Sakowski, from the Herkimer Pentecostal Church. I invited them in and they said to me they had heard our family was having trouble. "God sent us to you and your family. May we help you?"

They asked if they could pray with me. They presented the gospel message of salvation and even though I had prayed and signed the New Testament a few weeks earlier, which to me confirmed my salvation in a concrete way, I said the prayer again with all my heart. They asked me if they could come to the hospital the next day to pray for my daughter and, of course, I agreed.

The next day we arrived at the hospital and the guards came down that long, long ugly hall to unlock the door. Anna, one of the residents who was often at the door to greet all the visitors, came with the news of what was happening on the ward. As we began to walk towards my daughter's room, even from a distance it seemed all the demons that were tormenting my daughter from within began screaming and wailing. The guards came running demanding to know who these men were. Judy had stepped out so we took her back into her room. Once again they put her in the highchair in restraints. The pastor began to plead the blood of Jesus over her. At that moment, she began to scream so loudly that it seemed like the whole institution shook. Once again, a strange voice was speaking out of my daughter's mouth. The doctors and the orderlies came running as many of the other patients continued screaming. The authorities of the institution ordered us to leave the hospital grounds saying we had upset the entire hospital, their patients and not to mention my own daughter. On the way home, the pastor asked me, "You do know your daughter is not insane or having a nervous breakdown but that she is demon possessed?" My reply was, "Yes, I know." He asked me how I knew and I told him that from the beginning the Lord showed me that the only hope for my daughter was Him. Our only help out of this nightmare, the only one who could help us was Him. I told the pastor that when he came to my door and offered help, I knew it was the Lord sending him and God would do what He had promised.

When I went back to the hospital, I was met by a team of doctors. They said they examined my daughter and there was little to no hope she would ever recover and that she would have to be committed to the hospital for four to six years. At that point, they really wanted us to surrender our rights as her parents to make any more decisions for treatment for her. I told the doctor I already knew there was nothing they could do for my daughter and that I would never give up my right to protect her and pray for her recovery. I told them the only hope for my daughter's recovery was in the Lord Jesus Christ Himself. At that moment, some of them looked at me with such pity and even showed great concern but others thought I needed to be committed and was losing my mind as well.

From that moment forward, it seemed every time I went to the hospital to see my daughter, there was more scrutiny around my entrance into the ward, but I remembered something Pastor Welch had told me. He said when I went into the hospital, I was to pray and ask the Lord Jesus to go with me and plead the blood of Jesus. As I stood there holding back tears, that's exactly what I did. Every time I went, I knew more than ever before that the demonic world was real and that only Jesus could help us.

As time went on, my life was consumed with the love of Jesus and sharing that love with others. One day while visiting my daughter, my sister-in-law, Angie, came and I was sharing with her about the Bible and the love of God and the need for salvation. The next thing I knew my daughter was screaming and trying to choke me. I know some people do not believe in God's Word, but let me tell you the demons and devils fear and tremble at the name of Jesus. They know their destiny, which is declared in the Word of God.

Every time I had to leave my precious little girl in that terrible place, I had to come to rely on the Lord to protect her. There was one lady there who had murdered several people. She would not allow anyone to speak to her. They did not even have her restrained as she was able to walk around freely on the ward. Sometimes patients would try to speak to her and she would say, "What are you looking at? Do you see the blue-moon?"

I was learning to speak to the Lord knowing He world answer my every question, so I asked Him about this woman. "Dear Lord, this woman has murdered. She's already been sentenced and confined to this hospital. I am worried she may try to kill my daughter." The next day I walked into the ward and the woman, who never would speak to anyone, this murderer, spoke to me. She said, "I told Judy not to throw her food because she would get into trouble, but she didn't listen to me." I knew that my Lord was telling me He was protecting my daughter and He wouldn't allow anyone to hurt her.

God was about to complete what He had started in setting my daughter free. I had found out that the pastor could come back to pray for Judy, but we would have to take her into a private area. So with the arrangements made, Pastor Welch, Jerry and I began to pray. Pastor led us in a prayer asking that our hearts would be right, and we would forgive those who had offended us. At that moment, we called on the blood of Jesus to cover us. Judy was brought into the room in a wheelchair with a couple of orderlies.

As we began to plead the blood of Jesus over her, she slithered down into a serpent-like position. Her eyes were double the size that they should be and were jaundiced yellow. She first turned into a claw-like position and then screamed and tried to grab the pastor in an inappropriate manner. Then she began to speak in a seducing voice. "I know all about you." She began to say her name was not Judy but Julie and that Judy would not be back. Pastor responded all sins are under the blood of Jesus Christ. At that moment, her face squared off and totally became disfigured. She was not able to close her mouth. Pastor and Jerry continued to pray to the point where she was physically exhausted, and they returned her to her bed. Pastor said we would continue to pray along with our church that there would be a complete deliverance and she would be set free.

Later that afternoon, just before I was leaving, I was sitting with her in the sunroom. I knew in my heart if she would die in that state, she would be without Jesus. I continued to pray and suddenly she looked up at me. I called her name, "Judy!" She looked up and put her hand on her chest and in a seductive voice said, "I'm Julie, and Judy is dead." Suddenly something within me was released and I said to the spirit, "You are a liar, and I don't know how you got into my daughter's body but I know my Lord Jesus Christ will help me to get you out."

The next day, once again, I was at the gate waiting for the sound of the keys and the doors opening and slamming. I thought about having to walk down that horrible ugly, long hallway and the horrible foul smell of urine. I felt like I would never breathe fresh air again. As I got to my daughter's room, she suddenly sat up and looked to the bottom of the bed. She exclaimed, "Oh my Jesus! How could I have forgotten you?" I looked at her and began to weep because she was so thin and had lost about 35 pounds. I felt like this would be her last night on earth as I was standing by her bed. The doctor came in and told me they did not want me coming there every day. He said, "We have little to no hope for her recovery. The sooner you begin to accept the truth, the easier it will be for you to cope. We no longer want you to come up with your friends and disturb this whole floor. We have all kinds of problems with the patients. They all get agitated so, for this reason, we are limiting your visits." I was so totally devastated. I could not wait to get out of there to speak to the Lord.

I said, "Lord, I believe everything You told me that if I would believe in You and pray, You would hear and answer my prayers! Why God is she not healed?" In my spirit God said to me, "Oh ye of such little faith!" I went to sleep that night and I knew the Lord gave me a revelation of knowledge in my dream. I was in my kitchen sitting by the telephone and when I looked up, I saw my daughter standing in the doorway. She looked exactly as I had last seen her as I left the hospital that afternoon. I spoke to her and said, "Judy, you are all well!" She replied, "Mommy, call everyone and tell them that Jesus has healed me." I didn't realize at the time she was giving me the word of the Lord.

When I got to the hospital that morning, waiting once again to enter into the dark, terrible place, I didn't know if she would still be alive. I thought of the words Pastor Welch told me to speak when I entered the hospital. I asked Jesus to go with me and I began to plead His precious blood over everything. The door opened and Anna said that Judy was calling for her mommy. I ran down the hallway so fast and into her room. She was sitting up! As I ran to hug her for the first time in months, my daughter spoke to me. I knew it was her. She said to me, "Mommy, what am I doing here? Please get me out!" I knew by the Spirit of the Lord that she was truly on the way to total recovery. I cannot express in words the gratitude in my heart for my Jesus. I was resolved to serve Him for the rest of my life, and I've never regretted that decision!

When my daughter was released from the hospital and we were passing through Ilion, New York, we noticed Steve Fedele's restaurant. It was lit up so brightly and we could hear the sounds of people laughing and having a good time. Judy said, "I want to eat there!" The aroma of good food and pizza filled the air and was such a contrast from the horrible odor of that institution. I did not know, but God knew, that Steve was going to be like another son to me. We sat down to order and Steve came quickly to see how everything was going and when he saw Judy, his eyes began to fill up with tears. He began to ask what happened so I started to share the good news of Jesus with him and that Jesus had healed my daughter.

Everybody who knew Steve in those days knew he loved people and knew everything about everybody. Over the months of my daughter's sickness, Steve would check with me on the progress and what was happening with Judy. That night he sat down with us. I could tell that it was just another way for Steve to have a story to tell a lot of people because he loved dramatic events and had a large, warm heart. The Lord showed me that as a young boy, he was given over to Satan and had grown up in a life tainted by the world's perversion and demonic control.

I began to speak to him about Jesus and about the testimony of what happened in my daughter's life. Steve began to cry and received the Lord but the enemy was not going to give him up without a fight. Because of all the things that were happening in my daughter's life, I realized Steve needed deliverance from the life he had lived and the many demons who made their home in him.

I invited him to come to church with me. On a Sunday morning during the service, Steve started to manifest odd behaviors, shaking his hands and head. It became clear he needed to be delivered from demons. I told him that and he got so angry with me. Later that afternoon, Steve called me to tell me he had a knife in his hand and he was making pizza and something was telling him to put the knife through his chest and then to put his face on the hot bricks of the pizza oven. It continued saying, "See what your God will do." When he hung up with me, I called my brother-in-law, Sam, and my sister-in-law, Angie, and asked if they could go to his pizza shop and pray there until the time for the evening service and then bring him to church. I called Pastor Welch and told him as well.

When we got to church that evening, we were all worshiping when Pastor Welch said, "Is there anyone who wants to accept Jesus?" Steve raised his hand and was the only one to go forward to the altar. When the pastor put his hand on Steve's head, he began to behave in a somewhat violent way. Steve was an actor. He said to the pastor and the others were praying, "I'm just fooling around. I know what I'm doing," but the pastor and the elders continued to pray and many demons came out that night. Steve was on his way to being totally free to serve the Lord. As my sister-in-law and I walked home, we were laughing and laughing; Angie and I were filled with so much joy that we almost doubled over. We knew that the angels were rejoicing that Steve was becoming a son of God. Later that night, I was waiting to hear from Steve. About midnight, he called me and said, "Joanne, it was like I was in the washing machine. My whole body was shaking and the joy of the Lord came over me." Again, I started laughing and rejoicing through the night.

Steve and I became inseparable. We were telling everyone we could find about the power of God and His love for us. I was already having weekly Bible studies at my house so now Steve and I were inviting everyone we could to come to hear about Jesus. We were so radically saved and so in love with Jesus. We had no choice but to tell all that God had done for us and what He would do for them. We began to have a weekly radio program, *Light of Love*, where we would share some gospel music and testimonies. There were so many miraculous things God did in our lives. It was the beginning of a great move of God in the Mohawk Valley.

I am glad the Lord used me as He did and that I had the privilege of sharing Him with Steve and working with him and others to bring the gospel and the Holy Spirit to Central New York. We now see how God has moved using this early work to reach even the nations of the world. The Lord is faithful.

As many of you know, Steve and his wife, Rita, went on to be known as one of the most powerful prophetic ministries to the nations and continue to share the love that God has put in their hearts for people both here and abroad. Their children and grandchildren, I know, will continue to go on to serve the Lord as well. God is faithful!

Joanne,

I want to thank you for sharing your powerful testimony of what God did for you and your daughter. Through you, He opened the way for my salvation and so many others. Every time I hear the song, "Thank You for Giving to the Lord" (I was a life that was changed) by Ray Boltz, I think of you.

Thank you, Mama Servello, for being so faithful—I was a life that was changed.

Steve Fedele

Chapter 5

My Salvation

Joanne Servello's testimony of her daughter's healing is so powerful and marks the early days of revival in the Mohawk Valley. I can never say enough about how grateful I am for her patience and persistence in leading me to the Lord. My whole life changed and I started to live out my destiny. We are always on a path, just not necessarily the one God has planned. Once I was saved, though, I looked back over my life and I could see the many connections God brought about that kept moving me closer to Him. I still had choices but God in His mercy was always there waiting for me.

Though you have read Joanne's testimony, I am commenting here on my salvation from my perspective at the time. Being a small close-knit community, everyone knew of the tragedy of this young woman. The Servellos also owned the produce company where I used to buy produce for my business. Being a good Roman Catholic, when I made my order I would say to Joanne, "I'm saying the rosary for your daughter and praying to Mary for her to get well." Joanne would thank me and we would talk a little bit and that would be it.

The ordeal for the Servello family went on for several months to the point where the state wanted them to sign Judy over to their custody and the family would no longer have any say in her treatment. Feeling overwhelmed, cursed and broken for her daughter's situation, Joanne spoke to one of her neighbors who happened to go to the Pentecostal church. They asked if she would be willing for the pastor to come and pray for her daughter. At that time for a Roman Catholic to turn to a Pentecostal minister to pray was unheard of and certainly not welcome but because of the desperation of the family, Joanne agreed to have them come.

A few days later I went to do my order for produce again saying the same thing about the rosary. Joanne replied, "Steve, you can't pray to anyone but Jesus; it's only in the name of Jesus that we should pray. The Lord healed Judy and they're releasing her today!" I asked her if she wanted to go and get a bite to eat. She said she wanted to come to my restaurant. My curiosity was growing.

It was a strange and dramatic report. I didn't really give her any more thought. I went on with my daily work. Little did I know that her coming to my restaurant was going to open wide the door for me to step toward the destiny God had for my life. Sure enough later that day, Joanne, Judy and Uncle Sam Servello walked into my restaurant. Judy went immediately to the jukebox and played a song that was popular at that time, "I Haven't Got Time for The Pain" by Carly Simon. As that song was playing, something began to stir in my heart, that longing, that hunger I had when I was 13 years old when I went on a quest to find God. It came back as I listened to the words of this song by Carly Simon:

Suffering was the only thing that made me feel I was alive

Though that's just how much it cost to survive in this world

'til you showed me how, how to fill my heart with love.

How to open up and drink in all that white light

Pouring down from the heavens. Not since I've known you—

I haven't got time for the pain.

I haven't got time for the pain.

I haven't got time for the pain, not since I've known you.

I was overwhelmed with emotion that began to consume my whole being. I went downstairs to the basement of my restaurant and in the darkness of that basement I cried out to God and said, "If you are real, I want to know you." Those song lyrics were the beginning of my great awakening. The darkness that covered my life was being overtaken by the light of God's love. The words stood out to me:

My heart was filled with love;

and white light was all around;

and heaven came down.

My heart was filled with love

and white light was all-around.

And heaven came down

and I knew—I know you. Carly Simon

Even though I was moved by the events of Judy's healing and those song lyrics, the next day I felt strongly about staying away from Joanne and the things that she was talking about. At first, something was telling me, "You don't want this." But I was drawn

49

in; I took that first step on a journey of a lifetime that brought me to a place where I eventually accepted Jesus and asked Him to come into my life and forgive my sin.

It was like a tug-of-war in my heart and spirit. Thank God for Joanne's faithfulness. She wouldn't let up and continued to call and wanted to pray with me. I would find every excuse to put her off. I didn't want to hear anything else she had to say. Already many people in the community were beginning to gossip about her because she had turned to the Pentecostal church for help. They saw her in a negative light. Before her conversion, she was quite a colorful person and a local hairdresser. Joanne seemed the most unlikely one, by human understanding, who could ever be used for anything great, but for God. The one thing I could say about her was she was persistent and I thank God for that. She didn't give up on me nor did God who continued to work on my heart.

It's important to take a moment and talk about the Mohawk Valley and Central New York. We are always part of God's bigger purpose. It is never just about us and our personal journey. Our destiny, giftings and talents are always meant to be used for God's greater plan and good, the salvation of others. Over the years, we have seen God's destiny unfold and our roles become more defined.

Joanne was used to lead me to the Lord but within her own family, there were so many miracles that the Lord would use to bring many to His saving grace. The little Bible study, which she led, was the beginning.

Looking back, I remember that time when I was 13 years old and met Pastor Wilson and saw him with those visiting ministers who were from the West Coast and products of the early revivals. The picture is still so clear—the group standing before the little church in Herkimer, NY. I couldn't even dream of what God had planned; yet, through Joanne, we were beginning to see the unfolding of God's vision. In the years to come, each one of those people would play an important role in my life and in the church.

The plans that God had for me and the Mohawk Valley were birthed long before my time. About 1910 there came some evangelists from the Azusa Street revivals in California who were filled with the baptism of the Holy Spirit with the evidence of speaking in tongues. As they came to the Mohawk Valley, they were driving through Frankfort, New York which was a small village a few towns over from Herkimer. The evangelists saw two young men on the street corner in front of the bank. From their own testimony years later these men related that they were planning to rob that bank. It was the depression and things were very difficult. One man was Joseph Pileggi and the other one, Michael Massaro. Through the evangelists, these young men were converted on the spot, filled with the Holy Ghost and radically changed. I believe God intended to bring a revival to the Mohawk Valley. Mike Massaro ended up moving to Colorado where there was a larger Italian Pentecostal community, but he left a legacy here although the persecution was great in those days if you converted, especially from Roman Catholicism to Pentecostal.

Those missionaries continued to come to Herkimer, New York, where they witnessed to the founder of the Herkimer Pentecostal church, Mrs. Sakowski, who happened to be the landlady of Rita's first apartment on King St. in Herkimer. She witnessed to Rita and planted the seed in Rita's heart to accept Jesus. King St. was also the location for some powerful manifestations of the Holy Spirit. If you remember, that little, old Italian lady who lived near me and used to pray for me when I was little was also was saved in that revival. She would tell me I needed to accept Jesus. These all tie into the Servello family who were strongly linked to Rita and my prophetic calling. The importance of noting all the connections is to show the hand of God upon my life and His continual weaving of people and circumstances in His plan for me and the Mohawk Valley.

When Joanne had her son, Michael, she was very young and her husband's sister, fondly known as Aunt Mary, raised Michael as her own. Aunt Mary never had any children because her husband was killed in the war shortly after their marriage. Here is where the destiny of the Servello family comes in along with with that - my own salvation. Mary's husband was the son of Michael Mazzaro who was saved on that street corner many years before. His name was also Mike and Pastor Michael Servello was named after him. When Pastor Servello was 10 years old, Aunt Mary took him on a long train ride to Colorado to see her in-laws. It was on that trip that Mike Mazzaro Sr. laid hands on the young Michael Servello and prayed for him. I believe there was an impartation from the revival which was meant to happen all those years earlier and would finally come through his life to the Mohawk Valley. God was preparing a powerful work that Mike Servello and I would pioneer along with our wives and his mother, Joanne Servello.

Joanne really helped pave the way for the great move of God which was always intended for the Mohawk Valley. She was the most unlikely one, almost hidden, yet God called her forth for such a time as this. I believe with all my heart that no one, not even the devil, can stop the will of God. Joanne was so powerfully converted. She was an eyewitness to the sovereignty of God. There was no place for denying the living God, so she quickly began testifying and witnessing to everyone.

For sure, the enemy of the kingdom of God and the enemy of our souls will do everything he can to make it difficult to keep us from our destiny and what God has desired to do through our lives for His glory. Often, Satan will use people who are the closest to us to try to stop us. For example, when David brought the Ark of the Covenant back, his wife despised him because of what she thought was extreme worship. Remember, when you reach your destiny, it's not only about you but about those you're going to reach for Christ.

Because of Joanne, it seemed I could not escape! She would not stop and kept calling, inviting me to church and wanting to pray

53

with me; the more I resisted, the more there was a cry of my heart to be free. The day came when I finally gave into her persistence. Remember, this is from my perspective. I had never been into the Pentecostal church (I don't count the time as a child when I was tormenting the nuns). It was forbidden ground for a Roman Catholic. I wasn't sure what was going to happen and had heard some very strange things about what was going on in the church services. I just decided that whatever Joanne would do, I would do.

She insisted that we sit in the front row. The church was full that day. As Joanne walked down the aisle, she moved from right to left greeting people and waving, and so did I! What a spectacle I made of myself. You could hear people gasp. Pastor Welch sunk down in his chair. His wife Irene's sister told me a year later, "Brother Fedele, I must ask your forgiveness. The day Joanne brought you to church I said, 'My God, look what the cat dragged in!'" I said, "You should apologize to Joanne. She was the one who brought me—ha, ha."

Nothing unusual happened in the service. I thought it was nice, but of course, what did I know? The minute we got out of the church, Joanne said to me, "You've got demons, and you've got to be delivered!" My first thought was, *I want to slap her! I was a good Roman Catholic boy. If that's what she thinks, she's really crazy.*

I left to open my restaurant. Sunday would be a busy day. About 3 o'clock in the afternoon as I was cutting a batch of dough, suddenly, the knife began to turn towards me and I heard a voice say, "Go ahead and stab yourself. See what your God will do." I found myself facing the big pizza oven and I opened the door. I felt a hand behind my neck pushing my face towards the heat of the oven saying, "Go ahead. Burn your face and see what your God will do." Just at that moment, the phone rang, and yes, it was Joanne. She said, "Stephen, you have to come to church tonight." I told her what was happening, and truthfully, this wasn't the first time I had experiences like this—voices threatening or suggesting harm and other strange occurrences. Maybe Joanne was right about demons taunting me. She was quick to tell me that those voices of demonic spirits and were not of God. She went on to say that I needed to get delivered and set free from the evil forces harassing me and most importantly, that I must accept Jesus in my heart.

She continued by saying she was praying and interceding for me all afternoon. God told her that something was going on. I said, "Joanne, my restaurant is like an icebox! It's freezing and all the windows are frosted over." It was early winter and very cold outside but because of the size of my restaurant and the huge pizza ovens, it was always toasty and warm in there, but this day, it was like a freezer, dark and gloomy. Fear began to fill the whole place.

Then, something very unusual happened. No one called to make an order and no one came in to eat. Sundays were normally one of the busiest days. Within 20 minutes, Sam Servello and his sister, Angie, came walking into the restaurant and said, "We're here to intercede and pray for you and take you to the service tonight." From 3:30 until 7 PM, they prayed and interceded for me. I will be forever grateful to them for their love and faithfulness. Joanne was right. I had not really allowed the Lord to become my savior so I was an open target for the enemy. He wanted to kill me, literally kill me before I took that walk down the aisle again.

When we arrived at church; it was full. We sat about halfway down the aisle. We sang one or two songs and then Pastor Welch said, "Is there anyone who wants to receive Jesus as their savior?" Almost unaware, I was up on my feet and walking down the aisle. I was the only one who went forward. I knelt down in front of the pastor and three elders. They surrounded me. Pastor Welch said, "Do you really want to accept Jesus as your Savior?" I said, "Yes!" Then he said that we'll first pray for you to be set free. At that moment, I said, "You mean a deliverance?" He said, "Yes," and I laughed and said, "You know I'm an actor, and I can put on a performance for you as you've never seen before." He encouraged me saying, "Don't worry about that. We know what's real and what isn't." At that moment, my body went into contortions and I hit the ground in front of me. Then I would swing back and my head hit the floor behind me in a rapid continual movement. At that time, the pastor dismissed the congregation and told everyone to go home and intercede. The church emptied like someone yelled, "Fire!"

Years later Pastor Welch gave me this account: He said for about two to three hours they prayed and cast out six demons. Each was a battle. They were growling or speaking as they, the pastors, were praying over me. They would say, "No! We won't leave!" Finally, Pastor said to me, "Steven, you must renounce them and say you don't want them and in the name of Jesus, you want them out."

The ministry team continued to pray and command the demons to come out. I said what the pastor told me to say, and I meant it with all my heart. As I spoke those words, instantly the demon would come out and I would be set free one after another. But I had seven demons and one refused to go. There were even some physical battles and terrible things that the demon demonstrated. That wasn't the end but it was a mighty step towards freedom.

In 2000, a few months before Pastor Welch went home to be with the Lord, he finished the story of that night. Stressed, I got up and just walked out of the church, demon and all; it was a demon of perversion. As a young child my father's mother, a practicing witch, put some kind of curse on me. Sometimes, we don't realize the extent of what has been done to us or the longer lasting effects. The demon spoke his name but refused to leave and obviously, I would not let it go. This was a tremendous learning experience for my future. When praying for people who were demon possessed, I realized that a demon would not leave unless the person wanted it to leave. For me, that didn't happen that night but God wasn't finished with me yet.

By now, Christmas was approaching. It was a busy time of year at my restaurant. I cut Joanne off and wouldn't talk to her. I simply didn't want to think about it anymore. I made up my mind I was just going to live my life and do what I wanted to do. Needless to say, my life was in turmoil and increasing dramatic activity was happening around me.

It was New Year's Eve and I was sitting at a table with some good customers, and we were just talking. I was going to be closing early because I had plans to go to Albany, New York with friends. We were heading to some bars to celebrate. A woman got up to use the restroom. It happened to be upstairs. In a moment, she came running downstairs saying there was a man in the bathtub. My restaurant was actually in a house that had been converted to a restaurant. I immediately went upstairs to see who could possibly be in the bathtub. Sure enough, there was a man in the tub taking a bath. I said, "Who are you?" He turned to me and looked like a normal man. Then he smiled. His eyes were so deep with darkness and suddenly, there before me, he turned into the most horrible, ugly creature you could imagine. In an instant, there was a puff of black smoke and it was gone. Once again, the restaurant was turned into an icebox, a deep freeze. A horrible feeling arose and my customers immediately left in a rush. I know they felt it too. Just at that moment, Pastor Welch and his assistant came into the restaurant. He said to me, "Steve, you don't have much time. The demonic forces are rising to consume and destroy you and you must renounce that demonic spirit and be set free."

I fell to my knees and they laid their hands on me again to cast out the demon. There was quite a bit of demonic activity. You could feel the entire place come alive and after what seemed to be forever, the power was broken. As I renounced that demon in the name of Jesus, I commanded it to leave me. I was free. I opened my heart to the Lord Jesus Christ and asked Him into my heart. Pastor Welch said, "Steve, there's service tonight. It would be good for you to come and make a public confession of Jesus as your Savior."

A couple of my friends, who were going with me to Albany to celebrate the New Year, had to work until midnight. Our plans were not to leave until they got out of work. As I was getting ready around 10:00, such joy had filled my heart. I really felt free inside, and the idea came over me not to continue with my plans to go to Albany. I resisted that thinking as I promised my friends and if I didn't go, they had no way to get there. I just didn't want to disappoint them. I decided to stop into the church. and was there for about an hour and forty-five minutes. It was then around 11:58 and they were singing, *"...there is power in the blood, a wonder working power in the blood of the lamb."*

The pastor said, "Steve Fedele is here, and he wants to make a public confession and ask Christ to be his Lord and Savior." I walked to the front of the church and publicly asked Jesus Christ into my heart to be my Lord and Savior and forgive me of all my sins, to teach me His ways that I might live to serve Him.

Seconds after, people began to say, "Happy New Year! Praise Lord!" It was 1975. As everybody was celebrating and wishing one another Happy New Year, I slipped out the door, got in my car, and picked up my friends. We began our journey to Albany. I must say the roads were treacherous that night on the New York Thruway. Three times my car went into a spin where I lost total control and almost crashed. We could've all died but for God's grace. On leaving church, I grabbed two or three song sheets and passed them out in the car. We were five altogether and I began to sing the songs on that sheet. Everybody joined in. We sang *There's Power in the Blood* and *Just a Closer Walk with Thee* to name a couple.

By the time we got to the bar, which was going to be opened all night long, I think what I would call the conviction of the Holy Spirit began to work in my heart and my mind. I began to be very uncomfortable with the surroundings. At one point, I got up and I went to the bar and ordered a diet Coke. I was the designated driver. There was an elderly gentleman sitting at the bar and he looked at me and said, "Steve Fedele." I looked at him in shock thinking, *How does this man know me? Who is he?* Then he said to me, "Steve, a man of God should not be in a place like this. You need to leave now."

I was so shocked that as I walked away and came to the table of my friends just seconds later I said, "I'm leaving. I'm going to wait in the car for you, but I'm not staying in here." They asked, "What are you doing? What are you talking about?" I put on my coat and walked out the door. Fresh snow covered the street, and I looked for the man. He wasn't at the bar and there were no footprints outside the door. It seemed like he just vanished. I believe it was an angel that God had sent to me. These events opened my eyes to the greatness of God and His goodness and concern for me. I knew God cared about me. My life changed forever that night.

Thank you Jesus.

Chapter 6

The Price

There's always a price. What am I talking about? To move on, to advance in any way or dimension will cost us something. It can be as simple as setting goals to lose weight or save money. Those will cost time or effort to achieve success. The stakes can be higher with a relationship or any life-changing circumstance that requires something of us. To guarantee our salvation, our freedom, Jesus shed His blood and took the sin, our sins, the sins of the whole world upon Himself. That sacrifice cost Jesus everything. He endured all manner of suffering, torment and ultimately, a death that we might live. To make any serious decision will cost us something. Deciding to ask Jesus into my life changed everything. But, I wanted to know Jesus more!

After I received Jesus as my savior, I truly had a grateful heart. One of the first things I did was I brought a dozen red roses for the statue of Mary in my house and lit candles for thanksgiving for my salvation. My house was filled with Catholic artifacts, such as Saint Joseph, Saint Anthony, and baby Jesus as the Infant of Prague to name a few. My backyard was adjacent to the backyard of the Catholic Church. There was a staircase that brought me directly to the Church. I guess you could say I had a direct line.

The charismatic movement had already reached Herkimer and in my parish, there was a small group of people who were very sincere believers having prayer meetings. I decided that's where I would go, knowing that my grandmother would never accept the idea of me going to the Pentecostal church. One of the first meetings I attended, we were praying and suddenly someone began to prophesy but they said, "Thus says, Mary." I thought it strange but as Roman Catholic, she's the mother of God and certainly, she speaks to us was my logical reaction. I had gotten saved through the Pentecostal church, but I had every intention to remain in the Catholic Church and serve God to the best of my ability through the charismatic movement.

Joanne had already started a prayer meeting at her house and she invited me to come. She still asked me to come to the Pentecostal Church, but I said that I was going to stay at Saint Anthony's. Wednesday was the day of her prayer meeting, so I decided I would go. We were all praying and she said, "I'm praying for you and you're going to get the baptism of the Holy Spirit today." To tell you the truth, I didn't even know what that was. I didn't know if I wanted it, but there was something I was asking God for, something that I was ashamed of and very few people knew about. I could not read. When I was in school. I had many tutors, all who worked tirelessly. My Aunt Ella tried to help me but it was like a mental block. I could not read. Perhaps some of you would remember when as Catholics we were told we couldn't read the Bible. We won't be able to understand; we needed the priest to interpret it for us. But something in me was desperate to be able to read the Word of God for myself. I really went to the prayer meeting that day with the hunger to be able to read the Word of God. He saved me in such a dramatic way and I knew if I was going to really understand His ways, I had to be able to read the Bible.

At Joanne's prayer meeting, the atmosphere was always charged with the anointing of God. The minute I stepped into the room people were joining hands and praying. Many of them were speaking in tongues, but I cried to God in my heart and said, "Please let me be able to read your Word." Suddenly, I opened my eyes. There was a Bible on the coffee table. I picked it up and I began to read for the first time in my life. It was Psalm 23. Thank you, Jesus! Little did I know but it would be a roadmap to the provision of who God is not only in my life but all of our lives.

I knew Psalm 23. It was usually quoted at funerals so I always equated it with death, but in reality, it very powerfully speaks volumes about life. Within Ps. 23:1-3, we find the compound names of Jehovah in the Old Testament reflected in these verses. At that point, I began to study the Word of God. The Lord revealed to me who He is—the God for every situation in our lives. Ps. 23 opens declaring the Lord is my shepherd. In Ps. 95:7, it states that He is our God and we are the people of His pasture, His sheep. I came to understand He is the great Shepherd as seen in Mark 6:34: Quickly, I came to realize that He was not only the Great Shepherd but my Great Shepherd. In Mark 6:34, it says, "When Jesus saw the people (when he saw me, Steve Fedele), He was moved with compassion towards them (towards me, Steve Fedele) because they were sheep without a shepherd." As I started studying the Word, every name of Jehovah, our great God, reveals a provision for each of us to walk in victory with Him. Think of Psalm 23 and consider these names of the Lord and their meaning:

I shall not want—*Jehovah Jirah*—the Lord will provide; Gen. 22:14

Still waters—*Jehovah Shalom*—the Lord of peace; Judges 6:24 Restores my soul—*Jehovah Ropha*—the Lord who heals; Ex. 15:26

Paths of righteousness—*Jehovah-T-Sid-Kenu*—the Lord our righteousness; Jer. 33:16

You are with me—*Jehovah Shammah*—the Lord is there. Ez. 48:35

You cover me in the presence of my enemies—*Jehovah Nissi*—the Lord is our banner. Ex. 17:15

Anoint my head—*Jehovah M-Kaddish*—the Lord who sanctifies; Lev 20:8

With the seven names, comes additional understanding. The number 7 means perfection or completion that can only come through a relationship of truly knowing who our God is and what He will do in and through us for His glory. Everything in the Bible has meaning and points to the character of God who provided His only son that none should perish. (John 3:16) His plan is a perfect one and available to all.

As I began to read the Word, God opened it up to me. I realized I could not remain in the Catholic Church, especially in that charismatic movement. I had to go where the presence of the Lord was and where the Word of God was being preached. When I left the Catholic Church and started to attend the Pentecostal church, I began to remove every item of idolatry from my house and destroy all the statues and religious articles, but I could not bring myself to get rid of the statue of the Infant of Prague that my Aunt Ella had given to me. For those of you who don't know what that is, it's a statue from Prague of Jesus when He was an infant. The statue is dressed or shows the infant in royal robes like a king.

I returned Sunday evening from the Pentecostal church service to find the head of the infant of Prague broken off in the living room. I glued it back on only to awake in the morning to find it in the middle of the floor again. I quickly realized that His Word says I should have no other idol before Him. I threw it out.

By this time, my mother became an emotional wreck at my conversion and really began to spiral down into a deep depression when I left the Catholic Church. She wanted to put a guilt trip on me to stop me from moving on in Christ. The enemy, Satan by name, tried to use my mother to bring fear on me. She didn't want me attending more services in the Pentecostal church. That's when I began to realize I had to plead the blood of Jesus over her and over our whole house. Suddenly, there came a peace.

When my grandmother heard I was attending the Pentecostal church, she didn't hear it from me. She heard it from the Catholic priest who ran his parish with an iron fist. Even though he had retired, everyone still feared him. He called my grandmother to the church office and confronted her by saying, "You raised that grandson of yours and now he's going to that Pentecostal church. Get him out of there now!" Because some of the Servello family were already attending the Pentecostal church and Joanne was witnessing to everyone, the priest sent his housekeeper, Rose, to the church to spy and take down the names of those who were in attendance. I was waiting for the right time to tell my grandmother. I knew it was going to be one of the hardest things I ever had to do. I got the courage to go to her house to tell her but to my surprise, she met me at the door, stopping me from coming in and said, "If you go to that church, you'll never be welcome in my house again!" It was like a knife went through my heart. Then she said, "They're going to take all your money. That's all they want is your money!"

I couldn't believe what I was saying to Don Jenn. "If you make me choose between you and Jesus, it's going to be Jesus." She slammed the door in my face, and I walked away. Remember all that I shared with you about my grandmother and how much I loved her? She meant everything to me. But now nothing or no one was ever going take to place of Jesus in my life. My Aunt Ella lived with my grandmother and when she got home from work that day, my grandmother was dressed in complete black. Her hair was all messed up and she was rocking in a rocking chair crying hysterically. My aunt said, "Mom, did we get a letter from Italy? Did someone die?" She said, "No. Stevie and I are cursed. Those holy rollers! I cursed them but it backfired. He's one of them now."

She really believed it and she tried to break the curse off me but, of course, there was no such curse. I was set free from every curse; so after one week of being banned from the house, my aunt finally talked her into letting me come back. We had such a strong bond. She said to me, "Please, my dear son, can you wait and not go to that church until I die?" I said, "No. No, Honey." She lived another ten years. Of course, my prayer was that I would be able to lead her to the Lord. Over the years every time I tried, she would get angry, so I knew I had to back off. I prayed and had confidence in my heart that God was going to allow me to lead her to the Lord.

The rest of my family was still not happy with my conversion and break from the Catholic Church. I didn't use the greatest wisdom in this matter. Maybe I should've prayed and fasted first. I was so radically saved that I began to tell them that they needed to repent and get rid of their religious artifacts as well. I even said that in the Pentecostal church, the truth is being preached. Within a month of leaving the Catholic Church and taking such a stand against it, I was really forcing my family to turn against me and the Gospel of Jesus Christ.

Pastor Welch made an announcement that the following Sunday night there would not be a service at the Pentecostal church because we would all be going to go to Saint Anthony's Church. Yes, I just said that the pastor said we were all going to go to Saint Anthony's Church to the charismatic Mass. Immediately I went to the pastor and said, "Pastor, I just left the Catholic Church. I told my entire family that basically they had to leave it if they were going to serve Jesus. He tried to explain to me how the charismatic movement was an open door to the Catholics to bring them to Jesus.

I felt so bad that I had made such a commotion with my family that on the next Sunday morning before the charismatic Mass, I asked them all to forgive me and I pleaded with them to come to the charismatic service. I was uncertain of what would happen that night but among the hundreds that were there was my family though they didn't accept Jesus.

The service opened with singing "Heavenly Father We Appreciate You," but they weren't singing that to the Lord God of heaven. It was a film showing the pope being carried on his throne in the holy procession and everyone was singing it to him. I was so overwhelmed with grief in my spirit that I stood up and said, "Bull---." I walked out of that meeting with some of the other new converts that had been attending the Pentecostal church along with the pastor, the Servello family, and several others. It was at that moment we realized we could not go back. The Lord brought us out this far and it would cost to continue our walk with Him. Whenever there's going to be a move of God, a revival always brings a choosing of sides. One of the things I've seen over time is if we have a hundred people sincerely praying for a move of God, most often half of those praying for that move do not enter when it comes. Consequently, after the commotion I made, there were some fences that needed mending with my family members.

My grandmother had one weakness in life and that was she flirted with men that she thought were handsome. Well, it happened to be that Pastor Nick Welch was a very good-looking man. I knew if I could get my grandmother to meet him, she would warm up to the Pentecostal church. I remembered that she said all they wanted was my money. It was lunchtime and he came to the house and, of course, the minute she saw him she said, "Hey good-looking; are you married?" He turned beet red and said, "Yes, Mrs. Nardelli."

"Oh," she said. "Just my luck! All the good-looking ones are taken." Then she offered him a sandwich and he said, "No thank you, Mrs. Nardelli. I'll take a rain check." He said this because, at the time, he was fasting. With a loud voice she said, "Check! I only get one Social Security check a month and that's gonna last me!" Once again, he turned beet red realizing that she thought he was asking her for money.

Over the years, she grew fond of him and he of her. At my cousin's graduation, they asked him to give the benediction. Afterwards, he went over to her and kissed her on the cheek in front of the whole community. She liked it and was happy he acknowledged her. Slowly, with time and getting to know him, her feelings changed about that Pentecostal church.

In spite of everything that had happened, she was very proud of me when I became a minister. Years later the church had a TV program called *Upon This Rock*. When I would go to her house, with a loud voice she would come to the door and announce, "This is my grandson. He's on TV." The rest of my family did not quickly warm up to the idea of my conversion and leaving the Catholic Church. For many years, probably as much my fault as it was theirs, there were issues with my decision. But this changed when my cousin Margie was diagnosed with a very aggressive cancer.

The minute I heard, I drove to her home. I could see through the window she was on the phone. Her parents were there and her husband opened the door and said, "Margie, it's Stevie!" She said with some surprise, "I was just calling you! I want you to pray for me." She told me that she had watched my TV program every week. You could feel the tension in the house. The family really did not want me to be involved in her life, but she made it very clear to everyone that she wanted me to have total access to her whether at home or at the hospital.

At the hospital, her father made it known to the staff that I was her pastor and that I would have access to her at any time. This was a real miracle. During one of my visits with her, she said, "Steve, no matter what happens, I know that Jesus is my savior." I had prayed with her a few weeks earlier and she asked the Lord into her heart. She said, "I want two things most of all to come out of this whole ordeal. First, I want the family to respect you as a man of

God and second, I want the whole family together for Christmas Eve like we used to do when we were kids." She died on December 23 and of course, the entire family was together on Christmas Eve. At her wake, her father asked me if I would pray. It was such an honor. Thank you, Jesus. From that time to the present time, I've had the opportunity to minister in prayer to my family in a number of different capacities. This has meant so much to me because I love my family.

My grandmother's conversion was quite special. She was approaching her 90th birthday and she was in the hospital and had been for a while before her conversion. She suffered from blood clots, but this time it seemed to be more serious. On Sunday, I had gone to the hospital several times in between the two services, morning and evening to see her. I knew with all my heart that I had to bring her to a decision for Christ. Each time someone else in the family would come in the room, she seemed irritable about something. I thought if I push the issue, I might make her so upset she could have a stroke. I was fearful to really push it, but at the same time, I felt this urgency that I had to pray with her.

Finally, about 11:30 that night I went back to the hospital. Each trip was a 30 minute drive. When I got there, it was kind of an uneasy feeling. I saw no security, no nurses. It seemed like the hospital was empty. As I was walking down the hallway to my grandmother's room, I saw her. She had been ordered to be in bed. How could she be out of bed? I looked up and my grandmother was walking down the hallway. I said, "Don Jenn! What are you doing out of bed? She said to me, "A great light came to my window and I heard a Voice in the light say to me, 'Your grandson Stevie's coming. Whatever he tells you to do and say, you must do it.'" So right there in the hallway landing, I lead my grandmother to the Lord. She said to me, "Please don't abandon Ella. Take care of her and tell her that she must accept Jesus." Within days, dementia had overtaken her and for the last few months of her life, we really had no communication, but I knew that I knew she called on the name of the Lord. She was saved, so when she went, my heart was filled with sadness but also with great joy. It was one of those bittersweet moments.

The years that followed my salvation were marked by the choice to leave my Catholic upbringing and it brought divisions with my family that were very painful. Along with others who made this choice, I began to understand the price, what it would cost, to follow Christ. For me, it involved difficult times with my family, concern for their salvations and frustration when I didn't see them get saved right away. How faithful God is! His timing is never ours but what a joy when prayers are answered! My brother-in-law, Al DeCola was the first in the family to be saved and Al was only the beginning.

Chapter 7

Overcomers

So much joy filled my heart. I had been set free from a life of shame, guilt, disappointment but most of all from fear. My heart was that I would be a faithful Christian and share my faith with others, and I would serve my church and my pastor. This is what God put in my heart. No one told me this. I did not read it anywhere. It was just something that became real to me; something that I must do.

My restaurant continued being successful to the point where I had bought another building to expand my business. My conversion came right in the middle of moving from my old location to the new. That's when I decided I wouldn't have a grand opening. I would have a dedication service. Pastor Welch came and preached; the worship team came and this time I gave the food away all day long. That caught the attention of the local TV news station and as they were interviewing for the spot, they introduced me saying, "This is Stephen Fedele, the owner." They asked me why I was doing this and I stated that it was to share the good news that Jesus loves them. I had hopes that new people would come to church, actually, there were only two who came. They were Mrs. Mancuso and her daughter and that's when she shared with me what she had said to my grandfather in 1948 about a grandson who would bear his name and preach the gospel—even to the nations of the world.

At that point, Joanne and I were working together in the prayer meetings at her house. Sometimes we would have up to 100 people in attendance. We also decided to go to the local radio station with a Sunday afternoon program sharing our testimonies and faith. We had others share their testimonies as well, plus a lot of gospel music and preaching of the Word. We funded the radio ministry ourselves and the name of the show was *Light of Love*. On our way to the first program, I realized we had not talked to our pastor about this. I thought it was important to get his blessing and let him know what we were doing. Our intention was to advertise our church services and invite people to them. This might seem surprising to those who know my strong belief in order and submission to the local church ministry. Truly we had a zeal but without knowledge. It was only God's grace and mercy and the love and the support of Pastor Welch, who covered the prayer meeting and radio show, that kept us on the straight and narrow.

One of my greatest joys was when Pastor would order food at my restaurant. Usually, they would take it home to eat and of course when he came to pick up the order, I would never take his money. It was an opportunity to bless him and his family. The first two or three times he would pick up his order, I always considered it a great joy to see him. We would exchange some words. He was continually encouraging me. He would pick up his food and begin to go to the door only to stop abruptly, turn back around and walk back to the counter and say, "Steve, there is something I really need to talk to you about." Often, he would bring some type of correction. I appreciated that so much because it was in those times that God stretched me beyond my comfort zone to truly walk after Him.

Through all of this, it was hard to see the big picture. I was so grateful to be saved and so was Joanne. Sharing the gospel was the greatest privilege as far as we were concerned but God had a bigger plan and kept expanding our circle. I've mentioned, Michael Servello, Joanne's son. He was really resisting this message of salvation. He couldn't deny the miracle that had taken place in his sister's life. His wife, Barbara, quickly joined the ranks with Joanne and me. We would have regular prayer meetings at Barb and Mike's house praying for his salvation, but he wasn't having any of it. He came home a few times during the meetings and would become so angry, but eventually through the power of Jesus Christ, he was saved. Don't ever underestimate the power of prayer.

Mike and Barb had two sons. Michael Jr. is the current pastor of the church his parents, Rita and I and his grandmother, Joanne, started years ago; his brother, Joey is also a staff pastor. The church, which is now, Redeemer, in Utica, New York, began with Pastor Mickey Mingo. It was first known as the Mohawk Valley Full Gospel Church, and then for many years as Mount Zion Ministries. It took time for the pieces to fall into place but the Lord is faithful and His word is true—God had plans for the Mohawk Valley and they were materializing. We were excited and felt privileged to be a part of what God was doing.

77

Soon after he was born, the Servello's second son Joey. became very sick. At one point, the doctors told Mike and Barbara that Joey would probably not make it through the night. But God in His mighty power and mercy had other plans and he was healed. That's when Mike Servello Sr. gave his heart to Jesus. Within that same timeframe, Mickey Mingo, who was part of that group in front of the little Pentecostal church all those years before when I was a child, came into the picture. Pastor Mingo was part of revival meetings in our church. At a later point, he became our pastor, but at that moment in time, I don't think he remembered meeting me.

Mickey was a powerful evangelist and an awesome and outstanding prophet. In the fellowship of churches we were in, everyone was having him for special meetings. It was in these special meetings he called me forward. I was the first one he called. As I walked forward, I wasn't sure what would happen. He didn't call me by name but just pointed and said, "You come here." As I was standing in front of him, he laid hands on my head and he began to prophesy. It was the first time anything like that ever happened to me.

The essence of the word was *You are a rough jewel. I'm going to polish you and make you ready to preach my gospel. I will send you to the nations of the world, but I'm requiring you now to separate yourself from your business and give yourself totally to the preparation of my call on your life.* My first reaction to this was like Jeremiah and Moses—"Lord, I cannot speak!" I thought for sure he picked the wrong man. I could never speak for God. There were those in the church who were already very cynical of me because of my zeal for the Lord. They were always snickering and laughing. They wondered how could anything good ever come out of me. Truthfully, I was the most unlikely one out of all those in that meeting who would ever be able to do that. As with all words, they needed to be tested and confirmed. For the moment, I kept it in my heart.

No one could doubt that something was going on in the Mohawk Valley. In the early days of our conversion, we saw the miraculous in so many instances where God was moving in a powerful way. God was preparing a people and a place for His glory.

Often a word of prophecy is given for direction; it may show a glimpse of the future for encouragement or a guideline. I learned this calling—what God is saying regarding how you will be used—comes under the anointing of a powerful ministry and meetings where His spirit is present. The Lord comes into the meeting and people might drop to their knees and accept Jesus as their Savior if they haven't already. We began to experience these types of meetings and it greatly affected our little village. Events like this are described in the book of Acts which says because of this man, Paul and those like him, a community was turned upside down with the teaching of the Jesus. (Acts 17:6)

Already, God had been at work in our small village. There were several young men who had gotten converted and most were young people who were very popular. I believe it all hinges on those two men, the missionaries on the streets of Frankfort who years earlier had shared the gospel. Remember the back story— Mike Massaro and his friend, Joe Pileggi, planned to rob a bank, however, through those missionaries accepted the Lord and that changed everything, not only for them but for others as well (remember the Massaros and the Servellos were related by marriage). The early missionaries came to King Street in Herkimer, which was an area heavily populated mainly by Ukrainian and Polish immigrants. It was also a very strong Roman Catholic neighborhood. I had a first-hand account from two people who were involved in that original revival. The fire of God came down and people were saved up and down both sides of the street. God's presence was so strong that some individuals would fall under the anointing of the Holy Spirit. Yes, as hard as it may be to believe, there were people who rolled up and down the sidewalk, which is where we get the name holy rollers.

We were reaping the sowing of those early seeds and were beginning to regularly see salvations and miracles. One of the young men who had gotten saved was Bob who happened to live next door to me. He was a young man who was gravely troubled. He dressed all in black and was very Goth, living on the dark side of life. He carried that darkness with him. I witnessed that; I saw it with my own eyes. There always seemed to be something explosive happening in their home with one family member or another, but I remember an instance when there was such an upheaval, you couldn't help but wonder what happened.

Bob was eventually converted. He was so radically changed that dark presence was gone. All you could see was the light of the Lord shining so brightly. Without realizing it, we were stepping into the anointing fire of God that already had been established. It was just waiting for those who would be faithful enough to move in it and not let go. I say that humbly. It's important we understand as noted earlier, that there's a price to pay to be a forerunner. In every move of God, those who believe and receive face great persecution. You lose loved ones and more, but you must have a faith with a drive and a determination that nothing can separate you from the love of God. (Romans 8:38-39)

The Wednesday prayer meeting at Joanne's was a highlight in my week. I could not wait to get there because every week we had healings and deliverances. People were getting saved and filled with the Holy Spirit. It was truly a miraculous moving of the Spirit of God. On one Wednesday, I had this overwhelming sense that I had to go share with Aunt Zianest, who used to pray for me when I was younger and who still lived in the same house. When I told her I had gotten saved and I wanted to thank her for her faithfulness, she was ecstatic. I understood all those years earlier when she prayed for me that the work of redemption had begun in my life.

I had all the intentions of stopping in briefly, sharing with her and then leaving immediately for the prayer meeting. Nothing was going to keep me from prayer time! It was so powerful. Sometimes, though, we can become busy doing what seems to be good that we can become insensitive to the voice of the Holy Spirit. Little did I know that by stopping there to share with that precious lady what God had been doing in my life, a door of destiny would open for another person.

As I shared with her that I had gotten saved, both of us began to shout and praise the Lord. We sang praises to His name and she began to tell me that just that week two of her children had finally accepted the Lord, and she just received a letter from a grandchild who had accepted the Lord as well. There was so much to shout about and praise God for. Suddenly there came a knock on the door.

The old woman opened it and there stood her niece, Angel, who everyone called Bunny. She lived in the apartment next door and had known me since I was a child. Bunny was a few years older than I and was very angry and abrupt. She said to me, "Steve Fedele, how dare you come to my aunt's house and mock her and make fun of her like this." I said, "Bunny, I'm not making fun of her. I'm one of them now! I have accepted Jesus as my Savior." She said, "You what?" I said, "Yes, I'm a Christian. I accepted Jesus as my Savior." She said, "Can you please come into my apartment?" I said, "I can't stay now. I'm on my way to a prayer meeting." She continued, "Please, can you just come in for a few minutes. There's something I want to show you." I really resisted. I wanted to get to the prayer meeting but she was so insistent that I had no choice, so we walked across the hall to her apartment.

We sat at her kitchen table and she asked me a few questions. She said, "Wait a minute." She got up and went into another room and came back with a piece of paper. She handed me the paper and as I begin to read, it was a suicide note. She had planned to kill herself that afternoon. Immediately I said, "Get on your knees right now." I lead her in the sinner's prayer and she accepted Jesus as her Savior. She was my first convert. Her husband got saved and the entire family began to attend the church. She had an awesome voice. At one point, she did some nightclub singing but now she began to sing for Jesus.

Keeping the Testimony Alive

The power of God was so awesome in those early days that not a day went by that someone wasn't being saved, healed or delivered. They were precious times and the moving of the Holy Spirit was powerful. On Friday and Saturday nights my restaurant would close at 2:30 AM. and because the church was only a couple blocks from my house, I would always drive by it on my way home. One of those early Sunday mornings, I saw that all the lights were on in the church. It was in the middle of December so I assumed that maybe the water pipes had broken or that there was some type of problem. I stopped to see if I could help and when I entered the doors of the church, I saw Pastor Nick and his wife, Irene, dancing and worshiping the Lord. I walked up the aisle. They saw me and motioned me to come and join them. It seemed like maybe an hour but ended up being 2 1/2 hours. We had finished our time worshiping the Lord and we sat on the front bench of the church for a few moments. We all had to get home to get ready for church that morning which would've been in a couple of hours and I asked the million dollar question—"Why don't we do this in church?" That's when they gave me the hard facts.

As in the day of 1 Samuel 3:1-3: "And the child Samuel ministered unto the Lord before Eli. And the word of the Lord was precious in those days; there was no open vision." (KJV) Here is an example of the first generation that was so passionately on fire for God because of the supernatural visitation in their lives, but the second generation comes along and they haven't experienced it for themselves and for whatever reason the light of the Word of God begins to burn dimly. By the time the third generation comes along, there is a possibility of the light going out. As stated in 1Sam. 3:3, "And ere the lamp of God went out in the temple of the Lord, where the ark of God was, and Samuel was laid down to sleep;" (KJV)

We see the same type of thing today where a once vibrant church, on fire for God and sensing a real move of the Spirit of God, falls into the traditional patterns of man, having a form of godliness but denying the power thereof. (2Tim. 3:5-7, KJV) I don't want to sound judgmental or harsh but this is the cold, hard truth. Eli needs to be a warning to all of us. We must never lose our first love or take the move of God for granted or become ashamed of the move of the Spirit. We must be faithful to pass the testimony of the Lord on from generation to generation. The Bible says of Eli's two sons that they were very evil and ungodly, really the servants of the devil. (1Sam. 2:12-36) They disrespected the offerings made to the Lord and the office of the priest, leading evil sinful lives. They were so evil the Lord said He would make an example of them, and they would both die on the same day.

If we look at Exodus Chapter 1:1- 2, there is an example of three generations. Verse 1 states, "These are the names of the sons of Israel (Jacob; first generation) who moved to Egypt with their father, each with his family."(NLT) In verse 5 Joseph, a type of forerunner, was already there. I think it's very important that I mention this here. No matter how dark the times get, no matter how much the enemy seems to be working against the things of God, and the church is tried and tested, we know the outcome. The church, in Rev. 3:1-12, has a promise. In verse 3, remember what you have seen and heard. We are encouraged to hold fast. In Rev. 3:12 it says that to him that overcomes, will I make a pillar in the temple of my God. This is important as it comes in a word to the church in Philadelphia. They are acknowledged for keeping the word of truth. The name Philadelphia means brotherly love and here speaks to the idea of unity.[1] These verses clearly show the

---

[1] Strong's, 5361

importance of holding on to what we know to be true and the importance of the role of unity (love) in the church.

There will always be forerunners. God will always have a people who receive the word and contend for it. He speaks of those who will be overcomers—conquerors, who prevail and get the victory. Going on in Rev. 3:7b-8, this continues by describing them as those who have the key of David, (Is 22:22), those who have a servant's heart, good stewards of God's Word with the power of the Holy Spirit. They are the ones who hold the keys that open doors that no one will shut, and who shut doors that no one can open. In Rev. 3 the Word goes on to say that I know your works. Behold, I have set before you an open door, which no one is able to shut. I know that you have but little power, and yet you have kept my word and have not denied my name. (NASB)

Does this not describe Joseph even at his lowest moment? He never denied God and kept his servant's heart and the heart of worship through every turn and bend in his journey to his prophetic destiny.

We know that Joseph was sent ahead into Egypt. But the time came, when he and his brothers, along with all that generation (second generation) died; the Bible tells us that the people of Israel (third generation) were fruitful and increased greatly; they multiplied and grew exceedingly strong.

The third generation usually reaps the benefits and the blessings of those who went before them. This is probably the most dangerous time for the people of God and the church. Following this in Exodus 1:8, "Now, there arose a new king over Egypt, who did not know Joseph." (NASB) How could this possibly happen? Think about it. Through Joseph's dream all those years earlier, a type of prophesy of his destiny, God spared Egypt and the known world from famine. Surely you would think it would be recorded in their history that everyone would have known of Joseph and his ability to interpret the dreams for the king of Egypt.

The truth is the world and its systems continue to deny the power of Jesus even though all time is measured before Christ and after Christ, yet they deny the power of that name—the name of Jesus that eventually before whom every knee shall bow and every tongue shall confess as Lord. But the truth is it's not the world's responsibility to maintain the testimony of our Lord and Savior; rather, it is the responsibility of His people, the church. This is the result when we do not keep and pass on the testimony of Jesus from generation to generation. If we fail, the next generation will not be able to pass it on to their children. This was the result shortly after the time of Joseph and it continues in this present day. If we fail to keep the testimony of the Lord and his servants alive, how will others remember? How can we affect any change in our world without the testimony of the Lord?

Keep in mind Egypt always represents a type of world as an evil force. In Ex.1: 9-11 (NASB), the new king, who doesn't remember Joseph, acknowledges the sons of Israel are a mighty people and states he has to deal wisely with them or, "they might overthrow us. They might even fight against us." So taskmasters were appointed to severely afflict them and force them into hard labor. If we fail to do our part, we end up building and helping demonic forces gain territory while the church loses territory. Progress forward is stopped. The people of God forget who they really are and do not have the testimony of Jesus and what He has done, and importantly, what He would continue to do through His church if we yield and let Him. Rev 19:10b states, "Then I fell at his feet to worship him. But he said to me, 'Do not do that; I am a fellow servant of yours and your brethren who hold the testimony of Jesus; worship God. For the testimony of Jesus is the spirit of prophecy.'"

In Ps.78:3-4 (KJV), Scripture warns us to remember the Lord and what we have heard that our fathers have told us. We are not to hide them from our children but tell the generations to come of the praises of the Lord, His strength and the wonderful works He has done. Unfortunately, over time, we can lose our enthusiasm and fear what others think. It's easy to fall into a rut and not remember the Lord. Mt. 5:10-12 (KJV) speaks about being persecuted for your faith. We can be challenged when we keep the faith and face ridicule because of it.

The church today faces a great deal of ridicule. Years ago, Pastor Welch and his wife began to bring me to an understanding of that. There would be a cost for the precious presence of the Lord but it is so important that we keep the testimony of the Lord alive which will demonstrate the power, holiness, and the gospel of God in our present day.

Part Two: The Fruit of Destiny

Chapter 8

Laying the Foundation

No one is an accident. No matter what the circumstances of your conception or however horrible the situation was, even rape or incest, you are still a valid and precious soul with a purpose ordained by God.

In Jeremiah 1:5, the Lord speaks a type of prophecy: "Before I formed thee in the belly I knew thee; and before thou camest forth out of the womb I sanctified thee, [and] I ordained thee a prophet unto the nations." (KJV) The idea of "formed" communicates a kind of molding and shaping, something like a potter would do.[2] It is even pictured as similar to squeezing into a shape and fashioned for a specific purpose. We see in this verse that the Lord had such a specific purpose for Jeremiah. He was to be a prophet to the nations. That was hard for him to imagine. Maybe you can relate to that. What purpose could God have for me? God is not a respecter of people nor does He show favoritism. In my life, He called me to be a prophet to the nations but what did He call you to? What has He prepared for you? It's a process. Take inventory. What comes

---

[2] Strong's 3334-5, Heb.

to your mind? What has been on your heart? You won't have all the details to begin, but start to believe and take notice. You are here for a reason.

As you have already read, my communication skills were very limited. How could God ever use me? Often when people ask how I began to prophesy, I tell them it was truly because the Lord touched my lips and told me not to fear. I guess the Scriptures are really true where it says He takes the foolish things to confound the wise (1 Cor. 1:27). In the New Living Translation, it reads, "Instead, God chose things the world considers foolish in order to shame those who think they are wise. And He chose things that are powerless to shame those who are powerful."

God, throughout His Word, clearly demonstrates that there has always been a plan for man. Looking at Scripture, the people He used were all flawed, hesitant and often outright fearful of whatever God was asking them to do. Moses, Gideon, David and others, all contested God's plan. "How could God use me? You must be thinking about someone else? I can't do that!" Did you ever think that?

Obviously, you are not alone.

God is clear. He makes it plain; He didn't make a mistake. He knew what He was doing. In Genesis 2:7, the Word tells us that "man was formed out of the dust." Here the word dust means ground, ashes, even rubbish.[3] God can make something out of

---

[3] Strong's 6083 Heb.

nothing. This principle is demonstrated throughout the whole book of Genesis. What amazes me is God does this over and over. He takes someone like me or you that everyone else would pass by and never even consider and makes us a vessel of honor for His kingdom. We are encouraged by Scripture to remember what God has done for us. We need to believe what Scripture tells us. Consider the precious gift of Jesus, His son. "For God so loved the world that He gave His one and only Son, that whoever believes in Him shall not perish but have eternal life." (John 3:16; NIV) The word perish is used here and in the Hebrew, it speaks of leaving behind.[4] God is not leaving you behind!

I have mentioned before that I could relate to Timothy's life. In 1 Cor.:16:10, Timothy is a good example. He was somewhat sickly or frail and brought up by his mother and grandmother. Paul held Timothy in high regard for his faithfulness and his friendship. Timothy was far from perfect in many ways, but his heart was right. He was carrying on the work of the Lord. Scripture shows us that life isn't easy but anything with any value comes with a price. Know this, we will be tested. Deut. 8:2 states how the Lord led His people through the wilderness testing them to see what was in their hearts. Would they stay the course? Would they be obedient? It was a heart matter and so is achieving our destiny. Believing God and

---

[4] Strong's, 622

remembering the Word is critical. Our next task is to begin to assess ourselves and our own life. Be ready to move forward with wisdom.

It will take courage to walk out your destiny. Fear is repeatedly mentioned in the Bible. The command is always, "Fear not." God commanded Joshua in Chapter 1:9, "This is my command—be strong and courageous! Do not be afraid or discouraged. For the Lord your God is with you wherever you go." (NLT) The word strong in this instance in Hebrew refers to being fastened or to fasten.[5] Think about that. Fasten your strength, almost as putting on the armor of God. (Eph. 6:11) Hold on to it!

Going on in 2 Tim. 1:7 God says, "For God has not given us a spirit of fear and timidity, but of power, love, and self-discipline." (NLT) Let's take a look at that contrast between fear and timidity and consider the elements in the second part of the verse—power, love and a sound mind.

The word fear in Greek refers to bondage.[6] A Christian, who has Christ in his heart and has the Spirit of God within him, does not need to walk in fear. The Word vehemently states, fear not! Fear not the face of man or fear not the dangers you encounter. For example take the apostle, Paul; he faced many instances of danger noted in 2 Cor.11:26. His response is: "None of these things move me." (Acts 20:24 NKJ) Ironically, Paul's name actually means,

---

[5] Strong's Concordance, 2388
[6] Strong's

94

little or humble.[7] Think about that! A man who most would consider an amazingly strong figure, speaks of the dangers he faced, and in I Tim. 1:15 he calls himself not only a sinner but the chief sinner. (KJV) When pursuing God, we are to count it all joy when we face challenges. Don't let fear harass you! In Eph. 6:10, Scripture states, "Finally, be strong in the Lord and in His mighty power." (NIV) In Greek, the word power here refers to miraculous power.[8] Imagine that—not only power but miraculous power is our portion. God doesn't call us to a purpose and not equip us and make a way.

Our job is to start assessing our life and to be diligent to listen for His voice. It's important to stop and note that spending time in prayer is of the utmost importance. How can we have faith to believe if we're not spending time with Him in prayer and reading the Word? How can you learn not to fear without knowing the Word? If you're not doing it, start. Don't waste time feeling guilty, just begin. Build a habit. God will help you do it. As we become more focused on the Lord and His Word, He is always faithful to lead us and that precious time in prayer and reading provides the opportunity for God to speak. Perhaps, the most difficult part is to be strong and courageous. Dread not. Fear is real and we all have moments when we experience it. It's not that you won't feel fearful at times, but rather the question is what will you do during those

---

[7] Bible Lexicon
[8] Strong's, 2904

times? In Him, all things are possible. In Christ, we have the power to overcome fear.

The next element mentioned in 1Tim. 1:5 after power is love. 1 John 4:19 tells us: "We love him because he first loved us." (KJV) Even when we were still sinners, He loved us and that love drew us in and saved us. When we have that perfect love within, it will minister to others. This is the heart of God. John 3:16 is a well-known verse and says it all. God's desire is to see that none perish. A great price was paid for us so that we would have everlasting life. In 2 Tim. 1: 13 -14 it states:

> Keep and follow the pattern of sound teaching (doctrine) which you have heard from me, in the faith and love which are in Christ Jesus. Guard [with greatest care] and keep unchanged, the treasure [that precious truth] which has been entrusted to you [that is, the good news about salvation through personal faith in Christ Jesus], through [the help of] the Holy Spirit who dwells in us. (AMP)

The language is strong with "Guard the precious truth that has been entrusted to you." What is that precious truth? It is the good news about salvation through a personal faith in Christ Jesus. That truth is a treasure that manifests the perfect love of God. We are all individuals who have been created with varied skills, talents, and personalities, but we have one thing in common. Our purpose is to guard that precious truth and share it because of the perfect love of Christ, who wants no one to perish. Guard that good truth!

Consider the last element or attribute in 2 Tim. 1:7. It concludes with the comment that we have a sound mind. (KJV)

Perhaps at no other time in history could there be a greater need for a sound mind. We live in a world that at times, seems nothing less than chaotic. People not only suffer from fear and different physical challenges but ever increasingly from some degree of mental illness. In fact, statistics suggest that close to one in five suffer from mental illness.[9] So what does the Word of God say? For those who know Him, it says something quite different. We are told that we have a sound mind and not a fearful spirit and having the power of God within us, we can have what the Greek translation states self-control and discipline.[10] With the power of God, we can face the difficulties we encounter and see them through to a resolution. We can have understanding, clarity of thought and make good choices. In 2Cor 10:4 -5 the Word says:

> The weapons we fight with are not the weapons of the world. On the contrary, they have divine power to demolish strong holds. We demolish arguments and every pretension that sets itself up against the knowledge of God, and we take captive every thought to make it obedient to Christ. (NIV)

Walking out your destiny will take the power of God moving in you. Look at the language in this verse. Take captive every thought. It is a battle. You have the statistics on mental illness today. I am not saying that everyone who rejects Christ suffers or will suffer from mental illness. That's not the point. The idea here is we all have a life to walk out. It involves choices. It is easy to be

---

[9] NAMI, 2015
[10] Strong's, 4995

discouraged or feel overwhelmed or worse, but that's the time to focus on the love of Christ and the fact that He has a plan for your life, a good one. It may take a fight to change your perspective. You may have to fight moment to moment to change how you think.

In 1 Peter 5:8 Scripture warns, "Be alert and of sober mind. Your enemy the devil prowls around like a roaring lion looking for someone to devour." (NIV) It always amazes me how the world is ready to believe every crazy thing, but rejects Jesus and refuses or denies that we have a spiritual enemy, the devil. The Word of God presents a plan. God gives us a purpose and a direction to guide us into a fulfilling and satisfying life. We may fill out that role differently and walk unique paths, but the heart of it all is to honor and glorify God and share the good news of the gospel. Are you beginning to get the picture? You may think you're unimportant or think nothing good can come out of your life but God sees you differently; therefore, keep walking out your destiny even when you face the many challenges this life can bring, remember this—Is. 43:1-15 (KJV) says it all. The Lord tells us that He is God, our Savior. Before Him, no other God was formed (v.10); yet, He and He alone created us to specifically be His witnesses. (v.12) We are told more than once to fear not and that He will be with us as waters rise or the fires of challenges burn around us. He is with us.

The Lord clearly reminds us of who we are, saying that He made us, redeemed us and will always be with us even in those most difficult times. We are His chosen ones. Having said that, we have our part. In Jer. 18:1-2 Scripture states, "This is the word which came to Jeremiah from the Lord: 'Go down to the potter's house, and there I will give you my message.'" (NIV) If you continue in this chapter, the potter is at his wheel, molding, shaping and forming a vessel, even squeezing it out if you would. This presents such a clear picture of the Lord who formed us, is with us and patiently leads us in the way we should go. A potter would not sit at the wheel if there was no purpose. Consider that first verse which plainly states our part. We must go to the potter's house. We must go to the Lord. He takes our brokenness and disfigurement and makes something new, if we let Him. When that happens, our life cannot help but blossom, blessing us and others bringing about God's perfect plan. Later, we'll see this truth in the lives of Esther and Joseph.

When we have that relationship with Christ, we are on a sure path even when problems arise. Matthew 7:24-25 speaks about the two houses—one on the sand, the other on the rock. Have you ever noticed that the same elements of life hit both equally but one stood and one fell? The rain, the flooding, and the wind destroy the house built on sand, but in verse 25 the house on the rock, which is a type of Christ, did not fall for it was sturdy. Of course, the one on sand shifts and by the elements of nature is destroyed.

We can only begin to find our destiny when we come to Christ, bringing Him the good and the bad, surrendering all. He will establish us and when the winds of adversity come, as that great hymn states, we shall not be moved. This is the key to controlling and facing our fears.

In Jer. 29:11, once again the Lord declares a type of prophetic statement to all of us. I like to look at this verse in different translations.

In the NIV, "For I know the plans I have for you," declares the Lord, "plans to prosper you and not to harm you, plans to give you hope and a future." God doesn't want to harm us or do evil against us. Let's look at another version. "For I know the plans I have for you," says the Lord. "They are plans for good and not for disaster, to give you a future and a hope." (NLT)

Let that verse become real for you. Say your name as I have: "I know the thoughts and plans I have for you, Steve, thoughts of blessing and prosperity." It goes on in verse 12-14, "In those days when you pray, I will listen. You will find me when you seek me if you look for me in earnest. Yes, says the Lord, I will be found by you, and I will end your slavery and restore your fortunes; I will gather you out of the nations where I sent you and bring you back home again to your own land." (TLB)

That is God's gift to us, a hopeful future and expected end. It means no matter what you're experiencing, just like Moses with the serpent in the middle of the wilderness, look beyond the serpent to the good Shepherd. Look beyond your circumstance to Christ. It's not that you bury your head in the sand and pretend the issues of life are not there because they are, but by faith, choose to look to

Christ who is the answer to the questions in your life. (Num. 21:8, John 3:14)

Know this. The enemy of your soul wants you to believe there's no future for you. He wants you to think, "Is this is all there is?" And if you think that, you'll begin to make decisions that will limit and ruin your life. When you have the hope and the expectancy that your life is connected to the promise of God, you'll hold on to that and you'll understand that all the elements of your life can come together for His glory and your blessing.

There is always more than meets the natural eye. In 1Tim. 4:11-15, Paul exhorts us to let no one despise our youth. Whether you are young in age or young in the Lord, He gives eight things as a guideline. Eight is the number of new beginnings. When you come to Christ, He will make all things new. In Chapter 4, starting in verse 12, Timothy says to consider these things:

> Don't let anyone look down on you because you are young, but set an example for the believers in *speech,* in *conduct,* in *love,* in *faith,* and in *purity.* Until I come, *devote yourself to the public reading of Scripture, to preaching and to teaching.* Do not neglect your gift, which was given you through prophecy when the body of elders laid their hands on you. (NIV)

As a believer and follower of Christ, you have a future. He equips you with power, love and a sound mind. (paraphrase, 2 Tim: 1:7) You have an opportunity to walk out your faith. The Word of God tells us to be an epistle read by all men. (2 Cor. 3:2) When others see what God has done for you, it can bring glory to God by drawing them closer to Him. Think of yourself as a testimony for Christ. In the Greek, the word epistle is even translated in some versions as a stamp or pattern for imitation. This develops further. We are as a strengthened form or something to be shaped[11] such as with a cudgel, a synonym for a hammer. This enforces the idea of God's plan shaping/forming our lives. If you take nothing else from this know that God formed you for a reason. We are shaped by our choices, but He has a path for us. If we seek Him, He will lead us in the way we should go.

In John 13:34-35, the Word shows us one of the most important things we need to do. "So now I am giving you a new commandment: Love each other. Just as I have loved you, you should love each other. Your love for one another will prove to the world that you are my disciples." (NLT) The book of second Timothy is instructive in the characteristics that we are given and how we are to allow those elements to work in us as we walk out our lives. Here is a final statement that is both instructional and a warning: 2 Tim. 3:14, "You, however, continue in the things you have learned and become convinced of, knowing from whom you have learned them," (NASB)

God thoroughly equips. We are not lacking in what it will take to walk out the plan He has for us. As we do, we are models when our conduct reflects faith, love, purity and a willingness to share

---

[11] Strong's, 5179-5180a

the good news with others. We are positioning ourselves for God to move in and through us bringing about destiny.

All the above is the preparation. Many times people say, "I don't know what God wants me to do." One thing for sure, He will always let you know. I don't want to make light of anybody's life or pain that you've suffered because it's real to you, but you can't live in the past or in that hurt. I often say to people if you're looking back you will not be able to see where you're going. Take that inventory. Take some steps forward. Go for God

Chapter 9

Esther and Joseph

The Word of God provides many examples of people who experienced pain and suffering and had to work through challenges to achieve their destiny. These were real people who had serious problems and heartaches. One such person was a young girl named Esther who was an orphan. Could there be anything harder than starting your life as a helpless infant having no parents? (Esther 2:7). A cousin, Mordecai, takes Esther in and treats her as his own daughter.

As the years pass, the Jews had been taken captive and carried away from Jerusalem. King Xerxes had his own troubles with his wife, Queen Vashti. After ignoring a command of the king, the royal advisors told King Xerxes that she must be punished so other women in the kingdom would not follow her behavior. Their suggestion was to find a beautiful young woman to replace her. Many young women were brought to the palace including Esther. She was now at the door of her destiny. Mordecai warned Esther not to speak of her family and Jewish background. Her beauty was undeniable and the king eventually chose Esther above all others. (Esther 2:17) This led to a pampered life for the once poor, orphan girl.

Esther was in a place many would desire. It could have been one where she surrendered to the things of the world forgetting her people and how she might help them after achieving such a distinguished position. When we are in a place of comfort or ease, it's important to be on guard and not lose track of the Lord and what His purposes might be. Ease can be just as much of a trial as suffering. Sometimes, it can be worse. Mordecai was a type of the Holy Spirit who guided Esther through her entrance into palace life.

We get so comfortable when we know we're saved and going to heaven, but I want to challenge you with this thought. I know the day, the hour, the minute, the year, I got saved. It was December 31 at 11:55 in1975; it was five minutes before midnight of a new year. If my only purpose for getting saved was to go to heaven, the Lord could've taken me and I could've celebrated 1974 in heaven, but that wasn't God's plan. We must complete our destiny and reach souls.

Esther had a destiny. In verse 15, though she was an orphan and adopted by Mordecai, her father's name is mentioned. Nothing appears in the Bible without purpose. Her father was Abihail. His name means the father is chief in the Hebrew[12] and in the Greek it means favor.[13] Though he doesn't appear as a character in the story, through no fault of his own, the circumstance of his death leads Esther to Mordecai who becomes a voice in her life providing guidance and direction that impacts God's people mightily.

Again, even the most heartbreaking and devastating situations can move you along a path that will bring God glory. You are part

---

[12] Strong's, 32-2
[13] Strong's, 2428

of a royal family. You have been fashioned for a purpose and have gifts and talents that you can use for the kingdom, even some talents you may not yet have discovered.

In Est. 2:21, just as the Holy Spirit in our life stays and watches over us, Mordecai also was guiding Esther. He overheard two guards planning to kill the king. He told Esther and spoke as the Spirit of God will speak to us. She warned King Xerxes of the plan. The plot was spoiled and the men were executed. Esther gave the credit or recognition to Mordecai. Her favor with the king increased, though she shared the credit readily with Mordecai. Power will test your character and Esther passes the test.

In Chapter 3, her story continues. Haman, the most powerful official in the kingdom, plotted against the Jewish people. In verses 1-6, you see that Haman had great power. He convinced the king that the Jews were a threat. They kept themselves separate and this could be a problem. The king gave Haman the authority to do what he saw as necessary.

The decrees were sent out to kill all the Jews, young and old, and all the women and children. (NLT) Haman was full of wrath against Mordecai and the Jews because Mordecai refused to bow to him.

Haman wanted them all destroyed. He was putting himself in a dangerous place. Haman wanted power and at that time he had the king's favor. Pride always comes before a fall.

Mordecai was overwhelmed with grief and sent a message to Esther telling of the situation. In Chapter 4 verse 13, he warned Esther that she would not escape the decree despite her position. In 4:14, a powerful and important point was made by Mordecai, "For if you keep silent at this time, relief and deliverance will rise for the Jews from another place, but you and your father's house will perish. And who knows whether you have not come to the kingdom for such a time as this?" (ESV)

What was Esther to do? She had much to lose. It was time for her to step out, to open the door of her destiny. A custom or procedure of the court at that time was that you could only go into the king if he extended his scepter. If you were to be so bold as to go into the king uninvited, it could surely mean your death. This would be a challenge for Esther but these were dire circumstances.

You can be certain there will be times for each of us to accept the challenge and step out of our comfort zones when the Holy Spirit calls. What will your response be? Esther did something that as a prophet I appreciated so much. She sent a message or a reply to Mordecai.

In Esther 4: 15 – 17 it states:

Go and gather together all the Jews of Susa and fast for me. Do not eat or drink for three days, night or day. My maids and I will do the same. And then, though it is against the law, I will go in to see the king. If I must die, I must die. So Mordecai went away and did everything as Esther had ordered
him. (NLT)

What did Esther choose to do first? She chose to have everyone fast and pray. She prepared herself before she went to see the king. When the king saw Esther, he extended the scepter and welcomed her.

Why do I think it's so important that she sought the Lord first before she acted? Without a doubt, it shows wisdom and secondly, when you know that you know it's God who sent you, then you will be willing to say what Esther said, "If I perish, I perish. If I'm destroyed and I die, I die." There's a boldness and freedom that comes to do the work of the Lord when you know that you know it's Him. Whatever trial or hardship you find on the way to your destiny, your purpose in life, you know that He's with you. There is no weapon that could be formed against you and prosper if Christ goes before you. (Is. 54:17) If Christ is for you, who can be against you? (Rom. 8:31)

As the story continues, Esther goes into the king and plans her own reception that will lead to the downfall of Haman. The people of God are spared as Haman has no knowledge of Queen Esther's heritage. His plan to kill Mordecai fails and he, in turn, is hanged on the very gallows he had prepared for Mordecai's end. It's important here to understand that reaching your destiny is not just about your salvation but it's about the souls you reach and help find Christ.

The king realizes it was Mordecai who stopped a plot against him. In Chapter 10, Mordecai was put in a place of great authority and became a blessing to the Jewish people. Mordecai is a type of the Holy Spirit and could have done it without Esther, but He chose to use her just as He chooses to use each of us.

Joseph

Joseph's life began so much differently than Esther's. We could say he was born with a silver spoon in his mouth; however, Joseph was not spared the trials and tribulations of this world either. In Gen. 37:3, the Word of God says that his father loved him more than all his other brothers. Keep in mind he was just seventeen years old when the saga begins. In verse three of that chapter, we clearly see that Joseph was the favorite. His father had a beautiful coat of many colors made for him. You could see Joseph coming from afar in that coat. He stood out and was blessed. His brothers easily could sense the favoritism of their father towards him and they hated their brother. That hate reflected the evil Joseph would encounter because of his sibling's jealousy. Joseph didn't help himself when he told his brothers in verse 5 that he had a dream about them. Here sheaves were used to create a picture. His stood upright while theirs were tied, bundled and bowing down. Sheaves were used to demonstrate submission to Joseph. Their hate grew. He worsened things with the telling of a second dream even more inflaming when he clearly explains how in this dream his family bowed down to him.

The jealousy and bitterness increased. These are very dangerous emotions that can only create problems for anyone who lets them take over as did Joseph's brothers. His story has many warnings but how his brothers treated him is clearly an example of jealousy that can come back on you when it is unchecked. Perhaps as with Mordecai, who encouraged Esther to hold her tongue and not speak of her heritage right away, Joseph should have held his tongue, but he didn't. His brothers were outraged that their younger brother would brag and claim how in the dream, he had dominion over them. They conspired treacherously against him (v 18).

When things in our life turn ugly, sometimes even those who seem to be the closest may turn on us. In Gen. 37:18-20, Joseph's brothers treacherously plotted to kill him. When they saw him coming from afar, they mocked him. They planned to kill him and throw him in a pit. Reuben, who was the firstborn, stopped them. He knew how this would affect their father and was reluctant to shed blood. It's important to know that Reuben was the son who should have had the place of favoritism that Joseph had with their father. The firstborn son in that day would receive all; yet, it was Reuben who said that it would kill their father if Joseph died and encouraged his siblings not to kill him. On the father's deathbed years later, he still upheld Joseph's position and extended a blessing to Joseph's sons. Interestingly, he gave the firstborn blessing to the younger of Joseph's two sons. It is important to note there were many years in between when Joseph walked a difficult path while his brothers simply went on with their lives.

In the beginning on that day when they saw Joseph coming, the original plan of the brothers was to throw him into a cistern and leave him to die. They would kill an animal and put its blood on Joseph's coat and tell their father that a wild animal killed him. It is suggested that Reuben planned to come back and get him later. Obviously, the older brother was concerned about what they were doing. As Joseph approached his brothers, they mockingly stated, "Here comes the dreamer." (v. 19) Also appearing on the scene, approaching from the distance, were some Ishmaelite traders heading towards them.

When the brothers threw him into the pit, it must've given them great pleasure to strip Joseph of his coat of many colors. It was a dark day. Joseph's story doesn't end there as you know. The name of the tribesmen who brought him to Egypt, as noted were the Ishmaelites, which means God will hear.[14] This was the key that kept Joseph strong. He knew he heard from God and would not let go of the dream God had given him. He held onto that prophetic dream through the most difficult times in his journey. He would not forget that hopeful future he knew God had spoken.

---

[14] Strong's, 3458

This journey of Joseph presented many hardships and trials. Let's take a few moments and start at the beginning of the story and look at the names of some of the places that were a part of his journey. The prophetic significance clearly stands out. You will begin to see that what seemed to be an unfortunate and unplanned event, led Joseph to his God-planned destiny. There was an assurance of a purpose upon his life.

Joseph's father had given him a task—Go to your brothers and see how they are doing. His father sent him off from Hebron. In the Hebrew, Hebron means to have fellowship or join.[15] Joseph longed to be accepted by his family. A man finds him wandering and asks what he's doing. Joseph says he is looking for his brothers. The man said they went on to Dothan. (v. 17) In the Hebrew, Dothan means uncertain.[16] That's interesting considering all that is about to happen to Joseph.

The brothers were pasturing their flocks near Shechem. The word Shechem in Hebrew refers to a place of burdens.[17] For Joseph, that was surely coming to pass. Unknowingly, he was on his way to Egypt, which is often considered a type and symbol of the world. The world offers little mercy and many burdens.

---

[15] Strong's, 2266
[16] Strong's, 1886
[17] Strong's, 7926-7927
18 Strong's, 4079

Joseph was in the pit as part of his brothers' plan to get rid of him. It had no water and it was a desperate place. The pit was a symbol, like a well, deep but dry. Joseph, though, had a word. The Word of God refreshes like water. His brothers don't kill him, keeping in mind Ruben's warning. Some Midianites came by. Midyan refers to strife and contention. [18]The brothers sell Joseph to the Ishmaelites whose name we have already looked at, meaning God will hear. [19] In the pit, or in uncertainty or amidst strife, Joseph held on to the word or the dream God had given him. He was sold for 20 shekels of silver. Silver often speaks of redemption though it doesn't look that way for Joseph at this point. The brothers went on with their lives taking many different paths. A house divided against itself cannot stand.

While in Egypt, Joseph experienced incredible lows and miraculous highs. Despite all that had happened, he kept his integrity and God kept him. Life is a roller coaster ride. Some feel once they accept Christ, their lives will be perfect in every way and are soon disappointed. As has been stated, this side of heaven, we will have struggles and challenges. Holding fast to God and being obedient to His Word will keep us. We have His promise: "Let your conversation be without covetousness; and be content with such things as

---

[19] Strong's, 3458

ye have: for he hath said, I will never leave thee, nor forsake thee." (Heb. 13:5, KJV)

Joseph's journey could itself be a book, but we'll summarize to take it to the conclusion and see the amazing hand of God on Joseph's life. When Joseph was taken to Egypt, he was brought to Potiphar's house. He was an official of the Pharaoh and a man of wealth. The Lord prospered Joseph in everything he did for his master. The word prosper here means to push forward, to break out.[20] In Ezra 6:14, the Word says they prospered through the prophesying of the prophet. The Word of the Lord was over Joseph. Despite all the hardship and betrayal that he had suffered, Joseph never let go of the dream. The prophetic word to his life kept pushing for a breakthrough, to go beyond his circumstances.

Potiphar saw the Lord was with Joseph and that the Lord caused all that he did to succeed. (Strong's, 6743) Joseph found favor with his master and became the overseer of all the affairs of Potiphar's house. Eventually, Potiphar left him in charge of all the affairs of the household. (v. 5-6) Still, there are challenges. Joseph was handsome and the master's wife cast her eyes upon him and began to tempt him to lie with her. She was very persistent and this went on day after day. Joseph had to resist that temptation with the strength that can only come from a good relationship with the Lord. When he would not be with her, she cried rape. She lied and had

---

[20] Strong's, 6743

115

Joseph's cloak which she had been so brazen to grab from him. Seemingly in a moment in time, everything he maintained in his life for a good testimony was destroyed and he was cast into prison. In verse 21 of Chapter 39, it states "...but the Lord was with Joseph."

It takes some time and hardships in prison but later in the story it states that Joseph was put in charge of all the prisoners. The word all shows the extent of how Joseph was blessed even in prison. The story continues with how the Lord showed him steadfast love and gave him favor in the sight of the keeper of the prison. Joseph's influence and authority went so far that in verses 22-23, besides being in charge of the prisoners, Joseph oversaw everything and nothing was done unless he ordered it. The keeper of the prison paid no attention because he knew the Lord was with Joseph and whatever he did, the Lord would bless it. What a testimony! Think about it. He was in prison and the keeper, or what we may consider the warden, didn't even watch what he was doing.

In Chapter 40, the baker and the cupbearer of the King of Egypt ended up in prison. Both had dreams that needed interpretation and Joseph interpreted them. It was an unfortunate interpretation for the baker but the cupbearer was restored to his former position. One foretold death—the baker's—and happily for the cupbearer, the other showed a restoration. Joseph asked only one thing. Since he was still in prison, Joseph asked the cupbearer to remember him and mention him to Pharaoh. (v.14) That does not happen and more time passes. I don't mean to be cynical but let me tell you about advice I gave my son, Tommy and his wife, Erica when I ordained them into the ministry. "Always remember that every time you go to help someone at 3 AM with their marriage or a troubled child, do it unto the Lord. If you do it for people, they will disappoint you, every time." Serving a need rarely comes at a convenient time and isn't always recognized or appreciated.

In Chapter 41 of Genesis, the king had dreams and needed them interpreted. After two long years, the cupbearer finally remembered Joseph. The king was very troubled, so the magicians and wise men of the kingdom were called but none could interpret the dreams. In Gen. 41:14, Pharaoh called for Joseph and God gave him interpretations of the dreams. The dreams foretold of seven years of prosperity followed by seven years of famine. Joseph warned that during the years of prosperity, the king must prepare for the years of famine. Pharaoh was impressed and asked the question, "Can we find a man like this in whom is the Spirit of God?" (v. 38) He continued to proclaim that Joseph would be over all the land of Egypt, even the King's household.

Really take a moment and let it sink into your spirit how faithful our God is. If we will hold onto the Word of God, His promises and the prophetic word He speaks to us, God will bring us through our wilderness, that hard place, to our destiny. Joseph's earlier dreams, when he was seventeen years old, finally emerge. It was a bit of a process. He was not easy on his family nor was it easy on him.

During the famine, his brothers came to Egypt. Years had passed and they didn't recognize their long, lost brother. They certainly would not have expected one of the most powerful men in Egypt would be their brother. Eventually, Joseph revealed his identity, supplied their needs and forgave his brothers and father who came to bow to the man who supplied them with the food they so desperately needed. Joseph always remained with a tender heart and was moved with great compassion when it came to his brothers; this was the fulfillment of the prophetic dream.

I don't want you to miss the powerful point. The story continues and concludes in Genesis Chapter 50. Joseph's father dies; the brothers are moved with fear now because their hearts and attitudes were wrong even though Joseph forgave them and over the course of several more years, Joseph even provided for them in every way. Notice how they were always plotting together or whispering about Joseph. They never changed and at this point said, "Now Joseph will show his anger and pay us back for all the wrong we did to him." (NLT) Among themselves, they were all still guilty. They could have admitted they were wrong, but they could never bring themselves to say to Joseph that they were sorry. Instead, a messenger was sent to Joseph from the brothers saying our father gave us a command before he died. The message from his father was to ask Joseph to forgive his brothers. It still wasn't in his brothers' hearts to ask for forgiveness. Joseph weeps over the death of his father. The brothers, in verse 18, bowed down and said they were his servants. In verse 19 of Gen. 50, hear what Joseph said, "Fear not for am I in the place of God?" (KJV) Is there anywhere more powerful than to be in the place of God where you belong and where you will find your destiny? Joseph was there and if you stay faithful through the good, the bad, yes and even the ugly of life, you'll be able to say as Joseph did in verse 20: As for you, you meant evil against me, but God meant it for good in order to bring about this present outcome, that many people would be kept alive [as they are this day]. (KJV)

This is a verse often quoted and most people don't even realize where it is from. Finish reading the chapter. Joseph was moved with great compassion and promised to continue to care for his brothers and their families. He spoke kindly to them. It's important to note that Joseph forgave them, but we must always be ready to accept that the other person may never change or admit they're wrong.

Forgiveness is really for you. It will let you out of the prison in which you were placed. Whatever you do, don't forget to keep the testimony of the Lord alive and what God has done for you, what others have done for you. The book of Exodus, which is the very next book, opens with this being said, "There arose the king of Egypt who knew not Joseph." (v. 8) How could that be possible? How could that happen? Is Joseph forgotten? It's not up to the world to keep the testimony of the Lord or great men and women of God alive. That's our responsibility people of God, the church of Jesus. There's a price for destiny. It could be time, troubles or any number of challenges but look at just these two examples of Esther and Joseph. The lives of so many were affected by their faithfulness and God was glorified through them.

We know the children of God were enslaved for a long time. They didn't always remember what God had done for them nor did they remember the testimonies of those who went before. God in His mercy did not abandon them. Looking at the end of the book in Rev. 12:11 we read, "And they overcame him by the blood of the Lamb, and by the word of their testimony; and they loved not their lives unto the death." (KJV) Think about how powerful God says your testimony is. He puts it right alongside His blood. There is power in the blood of Jesus and it speaks to others when you walk out your destiny in Him. But walking out that purpose won't be easy. It wasn't for Esther; it wasn't for Joseph; it wasn't for Jesus, so why would we think it would or should be easy for us?

Chapter 10

Forerunners

To continue the story of destiny and God's purpose, we'll take a step back into my personal experience. Rita and I married and together sought the Lord for our destiny. Though there were many challenges, God did amazing things and in His mercy kept us on the path He had ordained for us. As we look for the Lord to lead us, He will. I am still amazed by all the things the Lord has done. In His mercy, He miraculously leads those who are seeking Him. Confirmations will come and doors will open or close. But in all of the twists and turns, we must be looking to Him, keeping in mind He has a purpose and a plan for each of us individually. He calls us to step into that divine plan which not only relates to us but always points to how we can be used to share His love and bring others to the knowledge of Christ as Savior. It's also important to remember that we don't see the whole picture at once. It's a process.

At the beginning when I first got saved, before Rita and I were married, there was such a hunger in Joanne, myself, Mike and Barb, and Pastor Welch and his wife, Irene. We would meet, pray, and encourage each other continuously. We became somewhat like an inner circle of intercessors praying for a move of the Spirit once again in the House of the Lord. Pastor Welch came to Herkimer with a real fire and desire to see something done for the glory of God. They saw many people saved in the church which grew to about 250. That was sort of the magic number if I could put it that way. It seemed any church in the Mohawk Valley that got above 250 fell apart. That's when all hell would break loose and bring division and strife. The churches then seemed to fall back down to 30 to 40 people who appeared to hold to the traditions of man.

I'd been walking with the Lord for about a year and I went to Pastor Welch and I said, "I have to get married." He said to me, "What?" He wondered where the conversation was headed but I said, "I want to get married." We both laughed. Up until then, I was afraid to be a husband or a father because of the example I had in my life. I didn't think I could do either of these roles. God was changing my heart but there didn't seem to be any young lady in the church who was in anyway interested in me. Maybe it was because I was so radical in Christ. I don't know that for sure but I realized I wasn't going to find a wife there. There was a Bible school not too far from my hometown called Pinecrest. I decided I would go there to find a wife—literally. I sat on the bench in front of the main building and watched all the ladies coming and going. I saw one young lady. It looked as if she came directly out of the holiness handbook with a bun on top of her head. Somehow, I thought she'd be the one.

She was a nice girl but I knew in my heart she was not the one. It was at that point I began to think about Rita. I just decided to call her to see if she wanted to take a ride with me to visit some cousins I hadn't seen in a while. I picked up Rita and took off for the day.

We had seen each other a couple of times since I accepted the Lord but it didn't go too well. Rita was a chain smoker and always had several packs of cigarettes with her. They were those very long thin ones and when she smoked it was as if she was waving a flag saying, "I'm independent." And she was an independent woman! One day I took a cigarette out of her hand and threw it out the window, but let me say I never did that again. If looks could kill, Rita sent the message that she didn't appreciate what I had done and I had better not try to control her. Eventually, the Lord delivered her from smoking and it wasn't an issue but she still was and is a strong woman.

That day while driving, we both began to talk about what we would want in a spouse. At the top, my list was a woman who would love Jesus and serve him. She stopped me and said, "I've got to tell you something but it's nothing to do with you. I did this for myself." She said, "I accepted Jesus as my Savior a week ago, but I want you to know it has nothing do with you." I knew in her senior year of high school, a friend prayed with her to accept Jesus but she said nothing seemed to happen so she forgot about it. When she was in college, she dated a guy and became engaged. He had become involved in Christianity, but they broke up. Now the timing seemed to be right. She, too, wanted to be married. As we continued talking, we found we shared other similar experiences in our journey.

She also had an encounter with an angel as I did that first night I was saved. On one occasion, she and a friend were on the way to a town that was having a psychic fair. This town was known for a lot of demonic activity. She was going with her friend and they stopped at a bar to meet up with other friends. The group was planning to go to the psychic fair the next day. She went up to the bar to get a drink. There was an elderly lady sitting at the bar who said, "Rita Nancy Spinosa, I know where you're planning on going and I am here to warn you there are evil spirits that are waiting to possess you. Don't go!" In a moment's time, she turned to her friends and the lady was gone. Praise God! Rita took that warning and she did not go. The conversations on that drive were bringing us closer together and that was not all.

When we arrived at my cousin's, we spent a little time talking and then my cousin suddenly said, "If there's going to be a wedding, I have to know. I've got to take time off from work and buy a dress. My sister has to know too!" On the ride home, we prayed and looked at each other. We realized that the Lord was putting us back together but this time it was different because we both had accepted Him and His plan for us in spite of ourselves. God's plan took the good, the bad, and the ugly to bring us to that place of His will for us.

Rita and I still did not remember, at that time, our short encounter at the college until 1972; yet, I mention this because it was part of the bigger picture of how the Lord leads even at times when we do not see the importance or outcomes of what appears to be chance encounters. We quickly put all our plans back into action from the earlier time when planning our life together. Still on the list was to be one of the great successes in the business world with the finances to be able to travel. As plans for the wedding developed, my soon to be in-laws began to understand that I was no longer the good Catholic guy. It was hard for them to accept and understand that Rita and I were born-again Christians, and we were going to get married by a Pentecostal pastor and in the Pentecostal church. Perhaps they were thinking, "Well, at least he's a businessman and there's a security there for our daughter." Their intentions were always well meaning. Rita's parents were the greatest people ever. I loved them both very much. On my side, I told Rita that I'd never be able to put my mother in a nursing home and that she would have to live with us. Rita agreed and as noted earlier my mother was with us until she went home to the Lord.

At the same time, Rita was busy finishing up her Master's degree while making all the preparations for the wedding. We were getting married on November 7, 1976, which happened to be a Sunday. On October 23, two weeks before the wedding, we were having some special meetings at the church. I got there early. Rita was not with me. No one else was at the church except one man. He was a little strange or distant. People say never judge a book by its cover but there was something about him. I didn't even say hello.

The church began to fill up and the meeting started. Pastor Welch was standing on the platform and said, "Tonight we have Prophet David Larkin with us. Come on up and join us on the platform." I couldn't believe it but this was the man who was in the church earlier, who was the visiting prophet. I sat up, nodded at him and smiled sheepishly. I was a little too late in welcoming our guest speaker. Later he preached and then he said, "I have some prophetic words for people tonight." My first thought was that I hope, my friend, Mike Servello, gets a word. It would be a real blessing to him, but sure enough, he looked at me and said, "Young man, come up here." I thought, Oh my God! I know that the floor's going to open up and swallow me or I was praying it would.

As he began speaking over me, he said these words, *Right now you're like a rough jewel, but I'm going to polish you and I'm going to make you ready so that you will preach my gospel. I will put my words in your mouth and you will prophesy. I will send you to the nations, and I will use you for my glory. I'm requiring you to separate yourself from your business now and devote your time to studying in the preparation for the call of God on your life.*

I know what you're thinking. Wow! It was almost word for word as the first prophecy (from Pastor Mickey Mingo) I received. In those early days when prophetic words were coming over my life, I just knew God had a purpose, yes, even a destiny for me. My life was beginning to align with God's plan taking the challenges along with the blessings and bringing me to the place where I'd be

126

able to say what Joseph said, "I'm in the place of God," and what was meant for evil and what was meant for harm, God will turn out for good.

The weight of responsibility began to fall on me. All day on Sunday I wrestled with the reality that my life was not going to be the way I thought it was going to be. All I could think of was Rita and all the plans we had made together. It was weighing heavily on my heart. I did not want to disappoint her in any way. I said, "God, this is no longer just my life." On Monday, I travelled to see Rita. It was a planned trip for some last-minute wedding decisions. It seemed to consume all our time but it was fun planning and looking to the future we would have together. But now, I felt like the weight of the world was on me. What was I going to say to Rita? We had resurrected our original plans from when we first met and I had said, "I love you too much to marry you," and everything ended. There was a part of me that thought, *What if Rita is not willing to let all our plans go?* Deep in my heart I knew I had to be honest with her and tell her what the Lord had spoken. I already knew in my heart that it was the Word of the Lord so when I got to her house I said, "Rita, let's take a walk." As we were walking I said, "Rita, I have to tell you something." She said, "Wait, I have something to tell you. Let me go first."

She said, "I know how much it means to you to have the kind of life that we've been planning but last night the Lord woke me up and He spoke to me. He said, 'Your life is not going to be the way

127

you planned but if you will yield to me and serve me, I will bless you above and beyond what you could ever hope or dream.'" What a relief and confirmation to hear Rita speak those words. In the future, the Lord would always seem to confirm a word to us. This was a great comfort especially in the days that were ahead.

The following Tuesday I went into the Herkimer Chief market to pick up my meat for the restaurant. The main butcher's name was Benny. He really liked making fun of our faith. He was surrounded by people who had accepted Jesus and he was agitated by them because the Spirit of the Lord that was with them. But when I walked in that day, he was unusually friendly, polite and even said to me, "Steve, my son wanted to be a pharmacist but he doesn't want to do that anymore. Do you know what he wants to do? He wants to own a pizzeria just like yours. And now that you're Mr. Pentecost, do you want to sell the business to me?" He offered what in hindsight was a pretty good offer. I said, "Where did you get that idea?" thinking to myself perhaps I should say, "Get thee behind me Satan!" When I got saved, it was a great joy to put my tithe into the offering every week. I really believed the spirit of poverty that followed me all through my youth was still trying to hold onto me. When it came to my business, I didn't even really pray about it. I had my mind set on a certain amount and his offer was way too low. The truth is if I would've accepted that offer from Benny that day, it would've saved us many problems. Saying no set off a chain of events from October 23 through January 23 that I will never forget. I went from making $1800 a week profit to not even having enough money to buy a small ball of mozzarella. The business began to drop almost immediately and continually went down each week until I finally closed the restaurant on January 23, 1977.

I did not return physically to the building until April thinking I needed to get it ready to put it on the market. Realizing that I had no customers and it would be difficult to sell after the long harsh upstate New York winter, I thought, *Now is the time to get the building and equipment ready to sell.* Well, I was wrong! When I opened the door, every last piece of equipment down to the forks and knives, everything, was gone. I immediately went to my neighbor and said that I had been robbed. I asked if he saw anything. He said in the middle of February there was a truck that backed up to the back door. They thought it was me.

Now all I had was the building! After several months, it sold and by the time I paid off the loan and the lawyers, Rita and I ended up with zero. There was nothing that happened in the natural that could've caused this to occur. My recipes and food remained the same. It was just suddenly no one was coming to the restaurant. Of course, Rita and I got married in the middle of it all and more challenges came. I was so consumed with trying to keep the restaurant alive that I had two car accidents to the point where at one period of time, we didn't have a car to drive.

Having no skills to do anything else, I ended up taking a job at a coffee shop in my hometown in a place that before this, I would never have worked. I was the short order cook and so where I was doing the cooking was open to the counter where the people would sit. When I started working there, I had to endure the mockery and persecution for my faith and of course hearing people say, "Where is your God now?" Most of the community was thinking the one-time poor boy who had nothing opens a restaurant; it's very successful and everything's going great; then suddenly he starts talking about God and loses everything. Sometimes, there are seasons when we are humbled and it seems difficult and unending. Rita and I had to take a Greyhound bus to her parents in Albany for Thanksgiving that year. Talk about being humbled. I couldn't help feeling, "What will my in-laws think?" Now as a father myself, I couldn't imagine marrying my daughter off to someone thinking that there would be security for her and then suddenly nothing. The God's truth is that they were loving, gracious and generous to us throughout all the years of our ministry. Rita's parents were a tremendous blessing to us in so many ways. I have told people over the years that I had the best mother-in-law and father-in-law anyone could ever hope for. I truly loved them, and I'm so thankful to God that they each accepted the Lord.

At that time, Rita had quit her job to complete her Master's Degree. Her teaching position in Herkimer was filled and there were no openings. She really loved teaching and it would always have been her first choice, but once again our God came through. She got a job at a nursing home as a dietitian. It was even within walking distance from our house. Two weeks after that, God moved again. My sister, Pat, had heard that the former owner of the newspaper, whom she worked for, needed a male attendant at his home, and so I was hired. It happened to be the first week Rita and I were both going to receive a paycheck. We had plans that with one check we would pay our bills which were many. With the second check, we were going to go away for the weekend. As you can imagine, we had been under so much pressure. We were just looking forward to having a little break.

We were living on about $25 a week for food for the three of us including my mother. I had gone through all my savings and all our wedding money to try to keep the restaurant alive to no avail. Many people had said I should go bankrupt. I couldn't because of all my suppliers. I had witnessed and shared with them when I was converted about the love of Jesus. For the testimony of the Lord, I could not go bankrupt. Remarkably, with the jobs we had, Rita and I paid off all our debts within one year and were even able to get a car. On the afternoon of receiving her first paycheck, Rita felt such a strong impression from the Holy Spirit saying to not cash that check. She heard, "I want you to sign it over and put it in the offering for the new church on Sunday." It happened to be that Sunday we were opening the Full Gospel Church of the Mohawk Valley with Pastor Mickey Mingo. Rita was thinking I was going to be so disappointed because we hoped we could go away for a weekend. This was around the same time, I received my first paycheck. As I put it in my pocket, I felt such a strong sense of the Holy Spirit's presence around me. I got this deep impression on my heart to not cash the check and just sign it and put it in the offering Sunday morning. I was kind of anxious to tell Rita what I felt the Lord wanted us to do with my paycheck. I picked her up from work and told her that we're not going to be able to go away. I said, "I really felt the Holy Spirit had told me to sign my paycheck; don't even cash it. Put it in the offering." She began to laugh and said that we're not paying any bills that week either because the very same thing happened to her. It's what the Lord told her to do. We stopped, lifted our hands and our voices to God and began to sing praises to His name. We laid hands on our checks and said, "Father God, in the name of Jesus, we give you these checks. We give them with all our hearts and sow a seed into the birthing of this new church for Your glory, Your honor, and for the saving of many souls!" Again, the Lord had spoken the same thing to each of us separately confirming His will. The following Monday, the superintendent of schools called Rita and offered her old job back. The teacher who had the position had just informed him that she was leaving and moving out of the area. The job was hers if she wanted it. From that day to this day, God has never failed us. He always supplied many times over in abundance even if to us the path looked different or unexpected. He is faithful! To God be the glory!

Chapter 11

The Local Church

This is probably the most difficult chapter to write. In the previous chapters, I've made some very strong statements about the Catholic Church but you could say that, overall, I had a rude awakening that there are no perfect churches. Pastor Layzell once said to me, "Do you want to have a church with no problems?" I was a young pastor at the time and my eyes got very large and I said, "Yes!" He said, "Then don't have any people!" Is that not the truth?

I would've been the happiest person in the world if I remained the pastor of that local church in Utica where we were sent to begin our pastoral experience. I loved being a pastor and God had given us such a wonderful group of people. It was only because of the enlargement of the call of God on our lives that we stepped into a trans-local ministry through a series of God-inspired steps that involved others and led to a great local team ministry that would serve God's people on many levels as we travelled abroad.

Over the years one criticism that Rita and I have received about our ministry was that we were too much in favor of the local church and of the pastors and the leadership of the church. I tell people, "That's a criticism I am willing to carry." And yes, over the years, I have heard many horror stories of people and how they've been abused by church leaders. I will share the experience that I had and

133

if not for the mercy and grace of God, I could've shipwrecked and probably never darkened the door of the church again. We must always keep our eyes on the Lord especially in times that are challenging or hurtful.

If we let offenses and disappointments stop us from serving the Lord and His church, there's only one winner and that is the enemy of our souls and the enemy of the Lord Jesus Christ, the devil. Scripture warns us in 1 Peter 5:8 which states, "Stay alert! Watch out for your great enemy, the devil. He prowls around like a roaring lion, looking for someone to devour." (NLT)

I believe it so important that if you've endured a terrible situation or incident that you must come to a place where you can give forgiveness, which is more for you than the one you're forgiving. Most often the offender would deny that he did anything wrong as did Joseph's brothers; after all he did for them, they didn't change, but because he forgave them, the prison they had put him in could not hold him. Again, it can be as true for you as it was for Joseph when he said in Gen. 50:19-20, "Fear not: for am I in the place of God?" (KJV) Is there anywhere better to be found than in the will of God? Betrayal is always painful but especially when it comes from the household of faith. Joseph goes on to say what was meant for evil and harm, God turned for good and for the saving of many souls.

I make no excuses for those who cause offenses or betrayals or church divisions; for sure, they will have to answer to the Lord for their actions and their words. (Eze.33:4- 6, KJV) Every time some-one got saved in my church, I would say to them, "I may disappoint you; I may fail you, but Jesus Christ will never fail you." We hear ministers say, "My church or my people." I have even said it but the truth is, they are the Lord's people. When I was beginning to step into the prophetic ministry, I was being mentored by some of the more powerful prophets and prophetesses of the last century. I was a young minister and I felt important because of this. After being in several meetings with them, I began to get a bit of a critical spirit and a bad attitude. How many know it's probably not a good idea to have a prophet with a bad attitude? I became very judgmen-tal of people from various denominations and the Lord was not go-ing to have any of that at all. One day, I felt as if the Lord took me by my shirt collar and said to me, "Do you see these people?" I said, "Yes, Lord!" He then said, "I want to tell you something, boy, you better watch out what you say to My people and be careful how you handle My children. Because if you mishandle My kids, I'm coming after you." Let's just say He really got my attention. I guarded my heart from that point forward and in truth, really loved ministering to people. The attitude was a typical youthful mistake.

Together, Rita and I always operated with much love for the people of God. As pastors, that was the motivation of our hearts and even after all these years, it's still one of the earmarks of our ministry. People will always remark how much love we demon-strate when we are ministering. If you're going to be a true minister of the gospel of Lord Jesus Christ and the people of the Lord, you better love what He loves. What does God love? He loves souls as John 3:16 states: "For God so loved the world, that he gave his only begotten Son, that whosoever believeth in him should not perish, but have everlasting life." (KJV) Christ was willing to do anything for the church. Though the Bible is speaking to husbands about how they should love their wives in Eph. 5:25 (KJV), the comparison is made between Jesus loving the church so much that He gave up his life for her. In Mt. 16:18 Jesus says, "And I say also unto thee, that thou art Peter, and upon this rock, I will build my church; and the gates of hell shall not prevail against it." (KJV) That's how power-ful the relationship and love of Christ are for His church.

I started off this chapter by saying there are no perfect churches. There's an old saying, "Don't throw the baby out with the bathwater." Some of you have already left church life because you've been hurt or disappointed by others. You thought your only course of action was to leave the church and separate yourself from them; that's never the right choice. I do not mean that you can't leave a church but you must always be in a church submitted to leadership serving and helping. Then the body of Christ, which is the church, will grow and become all that God intended it to be not only for your own development and training but most importantly for the fellowship of the saints. Don't let anyone rob you of that wonderful privilege we have in the body of Christ.

The importance of the local church cannot be overstated. There will be some negativity about church life but I believe the Word of God is very clear that the church of Jesus Christ is meant to be the focal point of all activity of the Godhead and will remain the focal point until Jesus Christ returns for His church, the bride of Christ. (Eph. 5:27) Scripture states that He might present the church to Himself in splendor without spot or wrinkle or any such thing that she might be holy and without blemish.

A common question that I will be asked is, "Why are there so many churches?" The answer is quite simple. The church of Jesus Christ is in the state of restoration. That means Christ is restoring His truth. In Scripture, there are original teachings and a pattern of what the church was meant to be. By the time Jesus and all His original disciples had died, the teachings of Christ began to fall in the hands of man. Can I say this? Whenever a man gets involved in the things of God, there's always a possibility of error. We must all agree that the Bible is the written Word of God, and it is the guidebook and inspiration not only for our life but for the life of the church.

History records the Dark Ages or Middle Ages as a period from about the 5th or 6th Century through the 10th Century. Why? Because much of the truth of Christ's teachings had fallen into the hands of men who developed a man-made system of religion. Most often this was to keep control of people and the extent to which they would be able to really believe in the Word of God for

137

themselves. The Word of God will always illuminate the path we are to take. In Ps. 119:105 Scripture tells us, "Thy word is a lamp unto my feet, and a light unto my path. (KJV) Not being able to read the Word and only having men filtering it, limited people tremendously.

As we stay in the Word of God, the truth will be restored. Through the Dark Ages and all dark times, and we can be sure dark times will always come, the truth will be revealed when there is a heart to find it. We also find in natural events and progressions in society and history, elements that can advance the restoration of truth. Think about the printing press and the effects it had putting the Bible into the hands of the common people. Think of how one historical invention affected the course of so many lives. Think of where we are now with technology and how that has enhanced our ability to get the Word of God out in many formats.

Hebrews Chapter 6:1-2 mentions the basic doctrines and demonstrates the progression in which each one will be restored:

> Therefore leaving the principles of the doctrine of Christ, let us go on unto perfection; not laying again the foundation of repentance from dead works, and of faith toward God. Of the doctrine of baptisms, and of laying on of hands, and of resurrection of the dead, and of eternal judgment. (KJV)

These are the basics, yet foreign to so many. It's interesting to know that every move of God persecutes or fights against the next move of God. The reality is the Devil can take a vacation because the body of Christ is at odds with itself. Perhaps right now you're in a church and praying for a move of God. You know with all your heart and spirit there is still something more and you're longing and looking for that. You are in prayer meetings and seeking God for a visitation from Him. What modern-day church history shows us and what some of the great men and women of God shared with me as well is that there is a great struggle with those who want to move forward and those who hold fast to the past.

Let's say there are a hundred of us praying, and we are all on the same page. You're praying for a visitation and a move of the Spirit of God. Modern day church history demonstrates that when the visitation comes and God begins to move, half of those who were praying for it will not embrace it and they will fight with everything that's in them against it. Those who do embrace it will find themselves having to move on and pioneer something new. The Word of God says in Judges: 21:25, "In those days Israel had no king; all the people did whatever seemed right in their own eyes." (NIV)

I believe before the Lord returns there will be an overcoming people who will be pursuing God; those who will not resist what He's doing in the earth but will embrace it and join with others to accomplish the Lord's purpose. Some of you are thinking how do I find the church that's moving towards perfection, unlocking the words of Scripture, embracing all the truth that God has already restored—a church which is open to the next move of what is yet to come? The reality of this is that there is no perfect church. The

139

church is in a state of restoration to be made ready for the coming of the Lord described in Ephesians (Eph. 5:27) as that church without spot or wrinkle. Here are the guidelines that I use for my own life and for my children concerning how we can learn to discern if a church truly has the hunger for all that the Lord has for us not only for today but until He returns.

The number one thing—they must believe the Bible in its entirety is the inspired Word of God and equally as important that there is no other way to the Father but through Jesus, the only son of God. There is no other name! Remember that's what Joanne first said to me. It's all in the name of Jesus. In Romans 14:11 it states, "For it is written, 'As I live, saith the Lord, every knee shall bow to me, and every tongue shall confess to God.'" This confirms that there is no other way; there's not a halfway house, nothing you can do on your own will allow you to earn it. We are told in Eph. 2: 89, "For by grace are ye saved through faith; and that not of yourselves: it is the gift of God. Not of works, lest any man should boast." (KJV) Salvation is not a reward for the good things we have done, so none of us can boast about it. The true church will exhibit the love of God. First, in Matthew 22:37- 40 the Word states:

> Jesus replied, 'You must love the Lord your God with all
> your heart, all your soul, and all your mind. This is the first
> and greatest commandment. A second is equally important:
> Love your neighbor as yourself.' The entire law and all the
> demand of the prophets are based on these two command
> ments. (NLT)

Further, in John 13:35 it is said, "Your love for one another will prove to the world that you are my disciples." The state of your heart and the state of a church's heart should be marked by the love of God both individually and corporately. This can't be any clearer.

Today, we can hear just about anything regarding salvation and what is acceptable to God, but the true church will hold fast to the Scriptures. Your salvation is not dependent upon an organization or a man. In Rev. 19:10, the Word states: "Then I fell at his feet to worship him. But he said to me, 'Do not do that; I am a fellow servant of yours and your brethren who hold the testimony of Jesus; worship God. For the testimony of Jesus is the spirit of prophecy.'" (NASB)

This was a reference to a man worshipping the messenger of God. Clearly, we are not to do that. Though we must respect and honor the ministers that God puts in our lives, we must also remember they are not to be idols before us either. I trust you really know my heart and I love the church and believe it is the vehicle God is using today and will continue to use until His return. Believing that, you can be sure there will be times we'll be tested. So often we want to blame God for the things that go wrong in our lives but I was one who experienced some of the negative themes that I've related. We've also discussed that God will use every experience to bring us to our destiny—remember Esther and Joseph.

The account of what I'm going to give you now is probably one of the ugliest times in my walk with God. As I just related, He will use all things for our good even the hardest of circumstances.

Rita and I were just married and we had returned from our honeymoon. Pastor Welch asked us to come over for dinner. He and his wife told us that they were leaving the area and taking a church near Rochester, New York. I felt like someone punched me in the stomach and yet at the same time I put a smile on my face and said how happy I was for them. I was really thinking about what was going to happen to us because, by this time, most of the church was not pleased with the progressive way that Pastor Welch was leading. He had been bringing more liberty and worship and of course Rita and I, along with the Servellos, were really his disciples and we were all in and willing to move forward.

It took a few days for the shock to wear off and they began to talk in the church about pastors coming to be interviewed. After the candidate's preaching, the elders would make a decision who would be the next pastor and the congregation would also vote. At the same time, I began to understand that those running the church were those of the second generation. They were good people but did not have the zeal or the hunger for the move of God as the original founders. They worked hard to erase the history of the church and how the fire of God came down in such a powerful way convicting and saving many souls. I'm sure as young children, they probably suffered a lot of persecution because of the move of God so to their credit the doors of the church were open and the lights were still on when I first began to attend. Some of them really reached out and were very friendly and encouraging until the day I gave a testimony about coming to the parsonage when I was 13 years old and the pastor and his family shared the love of Jesus with me. I told them the pastor's name was Wilson. You could see the reaction was not positive when I mentioned his name; he wasn't one of their favorites. Later on, I became friends with Pastor Wilson and knew him to be a man of God who would stand for the Bible. By then I understood the story of the church's history and it made everything perfectly clear.

After a pastor-candidate spoke at the service, the people would have an opportunity to say something for or against him. One candidate was a Bible school teacher and in the debate over these interviewees, one of the original members commented, "Remember what happened the last time we had a Bible teacher!" Of course, she was referring to Pastor Wilson. You could see the changes that were coming. The Bible teacher candidate did make a statement and said that there would be no more praise and worship on Sunday nights, which was probably the more liberal service of the week. On Sunday evenings, we'd have more flexibility and worship was livelier and there was a testimony time. The candidate went on to say that we would be having Greek and Latin lessons. I thought to myself I really wanted to learn the Bible and that would be great.

So when it came time to vote, I voted for him and obviously so did many others because he became the pastor.

We had our new pastor and there were some good and bad points to begin, but we moved forward. Mike Servello and I were very zealous for the Lord. We loved serving and doing whatever we could do. We found out the pastor had to be moved from the Bible school to Herkimer. Mike had his vegetable truck so we volunteered to go out and pack up the pastor and move him.

After a long day—a 3-hour drive going, coming and loading up the truck—we reached Herkimer and unloaded everything. Rita decided she would make a nice dinner and so the Servellos along with the pastor's family ate at my house that evening. Rita, of course, being a home economics teacher, had all her fineries on the table set for a king.

We were at the house talking and fellowshipping; Rita placed a huge antipasto salad on the table, but we were all still in the living room just talking. The pastor went to the table, sat down and pulled the salad to himself. He filled his dish and started to eat. No one had been called to the table and no one had said grace, but I thought, It's been a long day and he's probably tired and hungry even though he didn't lift a box or carry anything the entire day. We did it all, but our hearts were to serve, so I really didn't give it much thought.

When Rita called me into the bedroom, I felt a little uncomfortable. We had a houseful of company and I wondered what she wanted to tell me. She closed the door and said that man has

144

demons. I couldn't believe she was referring to the pastor. I felt like my head was going to explode and thought, *My God, I married a crazy woman. How dare she accuse the pastor of such a thing.* She went on to name the spirit in him and said it's lust. I thought, *Oh my God! What am I gonna do?* I really felt a bit of a panic. Rita was just newly saved, about eight months. What in the world would make her say such a thing? So I remembered—*We have a houseful of company.* I said, "We need to go out there. We'll talk later." I came out of the bedroom with a smile on my face and called everybody to the table. The meal was fabulous as they always are with Rita.

That was on Saturday. On Sunday morning, we went to church feeling good that we did so much to help the pastor and his family move. When he began to preach that morning, he said again that they'll be no more praise and worship on Sunday night starting next week, but there would be Greek and Latin lessons. This time it sounded different in my spirit, but I brushed it off and didn't think anymore. Still, I was very concerned about what my wife had said to me.

On that Sunday night, we had our praise and worship pretty much the standard, nothing really out of the ordinary. Of course, back in those days lifting your hands, or maybe clapping and shuffling your feet from side to side was considered quite liberal.

About two weeks after the new pastor was settled in his home and in the church, he called me on a Monday morning and asked me to come to his office. I was quite excited thinking perhaps he's going to ask me to be a deacon or Sunday school teacher. I walked to the church because I only lived a couple of blocks away. When I reached the church, he was in his office and invited me in. He asked if I liked this church. I told him I loved this church thinking he was checking for my loyalty. Then he said, "This is how it's going to be. If you're going to stay in this church, you're no longer allowed to stand, clap or raise your hands, sing, or give testimony." I said, "What are you saying?" and he said, "I'm sick and tired of seeing people watching you instead of me." I told him, "Don't you think you should talk to them?" and I left.

At first, I was a bit shocked but I thought well maybe he's testing me, and I always believed and still do that you should submit to the leadership of the church as long as they are truly teaching and following the Word of God. On the following Wednesday evening and Sunday morning, I did exactly what he told me to do. I just sat and did nothing. Of course, if he was worried about me drawing attention to myself, this was certainly a way to do it. My friends and everyone began to ask me what's wrong and I would just say, "Nothing; everything is okay."

On Sunday night, he once again was in the pulpit and reminded the congregation there was no more praise and worship on Sunday evening. But this time, it sounded like thunder—"There will be no more praise and worship on Sunday night!" About 100 people were in the congregation that evening but there's only five of us who will declare as eyewitnesses what I'm about to tell you. Along with me that evening was my wife, Rita, Mike and Barbara Servello and Joanne Servello. I have some very, very close friends to this day who were in the service and when I tell the story, they will tell me to my face that they never saw anything like that happen.

When the pastor was at the pulpit making that statement, you couldn't see it, but it was like a hand came swinging down from heaven and slapped him. We watched as his hair, head, and neck moved from the momentum of the slap followed by his body which landed on the floor about 5 feet in front of the pulpit where he had been speaking. At that moment, he looked at me and called me to the side. When I got there he said, "Please take over the service and lead us into worship." The one thing I'm not is a worship leader, let alone a singer, but I did what he asked and the presence of the Lord filled the church. All seemed well.

The next day, Monday morning, my phone rang and it was the pastor. He asked me to come to his house because he wanted to speak to me. The house was right next-door to the church. Once again, I made the journey walking from my house to his house thinking perhaps he was going to repent for what he said and how he treated me in his office the week before. I also thought that maybe he changed his mind about what he had said to them. Maybe this time, he would even ask me to be a deacon or Sunday school teacher. I rang the doorbell. He opened the door and took me by my shirt and threw me across the living room. I looked at him in such shock. Then he said, "What did I tell you? I said you're not allowed to stand or clap your hands, testify or worship. What do you think you were doing last night?" I said, "Pastor, you told me to." Then he said these words that seemed like I was in a tunnel and a freight train was coming at me and I couldn't move. "I don't care what he said. I told you that you could not do those things."

Yes, you're hearing me right. The pastor was demon possessed and the first thing I had to do was go home and apologize to my wife because I had really made her life miserable for a few weeks when she was the one who said he had demons. At first, I was so shocked and frightened to think that this could be happening. Who do you tell? What could I say? My wife and I began to pray and seek the Lord. I could not even bring myself to tell our closest friends, the Servello's. It seemed like the longest week of my whole life. Once again we were in the Sunday night service. The pastor went to the pulpit and once again the very same thing happened. He was slapped out of the pulpit and landed on the floor; once again, he looked at me and called me to come, but this time, I crossed my arms, looked at him and shook my head no.

Earlier, I related the story of the two men that were on a corner in Frankfort, New York? They were planning to rob the bank when the missionaries from Azuza Street witnessed to them and they got saved. One of them, Joseph Pileggi, remained in the area and pastored a church for many years but at this point his health had failed and he no longer could pastor. He was attending the same church I was. He was sitting in his wheelchair in the front of the church that night and he called me over. He said, "Steve, leave this church and don't come back. They will kill the Spirit of God in you."

Once again, the pastor tried to get me to come to meet him, but I told him I would not and this outraged him. He became so angry at one point he had called the headquarters of the church and informed them that I was a rebellious person and trying to cause division in the church. From the pulpit, he told the congregation that I would backslide within six months and Rita and I would be divorced. This is what I call a word curse or Pentecostal witchcraft or sorcery. It is when a Christian is angry at someone and in their self-righteousness begins to pray and prophesy about that person with malice, envy, and strife.

When someone prays in this manner, their prayers are like an arrow shot into the heavens but God will never receive a prayer in that spirit. What happens with that prayer? Where does it go? I believe that the principalities and powers snatch it and break that arrow in half. (Eph. 6:12) : "For our struggle is not against and flesh and blood, but against the rulers, against the powers, against the world forces of this darkness, against the spiritual forces of wickedness in the heavenly places. (NASB) More bitterness, anger, and violence will develop; one part goes to the person praying that which makes for more outrage and anger and the other one goes to the person they're praying against. That person begins to feel like something's wrong, but they don't quite know what it is. I believe

149

this is what the Bible is referring to when it talks about the fiery darts of the wicked. (Eph. 6:16) : "Above all, taking the shield of faith, wherewith ye shall be able to quench all the fiery darts of the wicked." (KJV)

In our ministry over the years, my wife and I have broken many word curses off people. Rita and I went into prayer. What were we going to do? There happened to be another Pentecostal church in town, a Ukrainian speaking church. When I went there on Sunday morning, there were only five members left, all about 90 to 95 years old and still speaking in their native language. I obviously knew this was not going to be the place for me to go. At the same time, Rita was at home praying and this was her prayer, "Lord, your Word says my husband is the head of the house. It also says that we are one; therefore, where he goes, I must go. I will obey your Word but now that makes You responsible to make sure that we are brought to the right place so that our lives are not destroyed."

The next day I got a call from Pastor Nick Welch. He said he was in town and he and his wife wanted to come to see us. As we were visiting, he asked if we would come to his new church and work as his assistants. I knew at that moment that they came to try to help us and we so appreciated them but the truth was we were not ready to do anything like that. Pastor Welch also said that we should not go back to the church. He didn't explain but invited us to go with him on the following Wednesday to a pastor's fellowship meeting in Syracuse, New York.

We arrived at the home of the general superintendent of the fellowship of churches. The Herkimer church that we were attending was a part of the fellowship and yes, even the pastor was there. He had told the fellowship that we were in rebellion. When the meeting started, there were about 30 pastors that asked Rita and me to come to the middle of the room. They wanted to pray for us. They surrounded us and suddenly the superintendent said to me, "You need to get off your high horse!" Then one by one several of them rebuked us for being out of order and rebellious.

They never asked us our side of the story or anything from us. We stopped attending the church, and we never spoke a word against him or the church. We had no idea what they were basing this harsh judgment upon. At that moment Pastor Welch stepped in put his arm around us and brought us out of that meeting. He apologized and said he had no idea that that's what was going to happen. Once again, he told us not to go back to the church. Rita and I got into her car to drive the hour and a half back home and all we could do was cry out to God to help us.

When we arrived home, Mike and Barb Servello were waiting for us and told us that the Lord had told them they needed to leave the church as well. It was at that point we related what had happened with me and the pastor. We all fell to our knees and began to pray, crying out for help from the Lord. At that moment, the phone rang and it was Pastor Mickey Mingo who called to say that the Lord told him that he should come to help us start a church.

We all felt like God had heard our prayer and began making plans not wanting to do anything to hurt the church which we were leaving. We decided to start a new church in another village but, unfortunately, within a couple of days Brother Mingo called me and said that he was not coming. Later he told us that the fellowship of churches forbid him to come. The phone rang again and it was Mike and Barb and they said they changed their minds and were going back to the church. Joanne had also left, but she was also returning.

So once again Rita and I were standing alone. Not wanting to hinder the Servello's walk in God, we told them that if we saw each other on the street for the sake of testimony of the Lord, we would greet each other but from that time, we would have no more fellowship because we did not want to hinder their walk.

One week went by, another Sunday morning, Rita and I were once again crying out to God for direction. There came a knock on the door and it was the Servellos. They were weeping and said we cannot go back to that church. We want to move forward with God; so once again, we fell to our knees and began to pray. Then the phone rang and it was Brother Mingo saying he still wanted to come if we wanted him and that he wasn't going to let anybody stop him from doing what God put on his heart. By the grace of God, we began the church called The Church of the Mohawk Valley. This was an incredibly difficult time but we were determined to keep our hearts right before the Lord. We trusted Him to lead us and He was faithful. We didn't see all the pieces at once but God in His mercy directed our path and heard our hearts' cry. He is faithful.

Chapter 12

The Power of the Holy Spirit

Pastor Mickey Mingo would play an important role in my life and help bring me to my destiny. Thirteen years had passed since that first time I saw him with Pastor Wilson and the others. I had just gotten saved, and he had been invited by the fellowship of churches in New York State to evangelize in our area. His nickname was "Wildman Mingo." He became very popular in our area and was a great blessing. Rita and I, along with the Servellos, quickly became Mingo groupies. As much as possible we would go to his meetings throughout Central New York. I remember one night I had arrived at the church late and there was a lovely lady standing in the hallway. I was very enthused about Brother Mingo and his ministry. I said to the lady, "Have you ever been in any of Brother Mingo's meetings before?" She said, "A few," and so I just wandered into the church and sat down.

That night as the meeting started Brother Mingo said, "I'd like to introduce my wife, Deanna. She is here tonight all the way from Seattle, Washington." Yes, you guessed it she was the lovely lady in the hallway. We laughed about this for many years after and even after Brother Mingo had gone home to be with the Lord, we remained very close to his wife and family. I love them very much for all they've invested in our lives.

When Brother Mingo offered to come and pastor us and start the church, it was a real blessing because he was so anointed and used by God. On Easter morning 1977, we began the first service of the Mohawk Valley Church. People quickly began to come as there was a great manifestation of the move of the Spirit. Because of his popularity in Central New York, many people came to our special evangelistic camp meetings. During these tent meetings, we saw so many miracles.

One miracle involved a very special couple, Steve and Marilyn Zuk who the Lord was adding to our church. Rita had a dream that Steve and Marilyn were killed in a motorcycle accident. It was so heavy on her heart she called brother Mingo to tell him. Rita and I did not know that the Zuks were going by motorcycle in about an hour and a half to talk to Brother Mingo about joining us. When Brother Mingo heard the dream, he told Rita to call the Zuks and tell them not to come. Thank God for his supernatural intervention in our lives.

Brother Mingo was a prophet—a very powerful one. I can honestly say after all these years of ministry working with some powerful prophets of the last century, I've never come across any who could hold a candle to the anointing and the power on Brother Mingo's prophetic ministry. As we were pioneering this work in New York, we would have street meetings where we would sing and rejoice and testify of the Lord Jesus Christ. Often people on the street would be overcome by the power of the Holy Spirit. We had a pickup truck at the location and would put people in the truck and bring them to Mike and Barb Servello's house where we would continue to pray for them to be delivered, saved, healed and filled with the Holy Ghost.

We had all been so radically saved and were on fire by the power of the Holy Ghost. In almost every service not only were people getting saved but were also literally delivered from demons during worship. These salvations and deliverances were a testimony of what the Lord was doing in the lives of so many people that the community began to see these dramatic changes which led to many more coming to the house of the Lord.

Herkimer had a community college. There were many college students who lived on the main street of the village where we would have our street meetings. Some would hang out their windows laughing and mocking us as we carried on preaching and glorifying the Lord. Others were on the perimeter of the meeting and the power of God would come and begin to saturate them in His glory and strength. Those college students would drop to their knees and confess that Jesus Christ was the Lord of Lords. If I began to mention the names of people, it would fill a couple of volumes, but I must mention two couples who are still in the church today. They were just young, single, college students in those days and today they continue serving and making a great impact on the Mohawk Valley.

From the start, Mike and Tammy Hughes and Howard and Paula Quick demonstrated true servants' hearts. They were a blessing to us and to others. Today, their children are walking with and serving the Lord, the next generation. They are the perfect demonstration of the power and influence of the local church on lives. As you look at Redeemer today, the church that grew out of our small group, it is a multigenerational and multicultural church which is a testimony to those who allowed themselves to be planted and committed to serving the ministry and their communities. Their foundation is the Rock, Jesus, our Lord and Savior. Through their commitment, their families' roots went down deep and their children became a part of the vision and now serve with their own young children. It is hard to even comprehend how much has grown out of that small group and that little Bible study.

At that time, our Wednesday prayer meetings continued as did our weekly radio show. They were catalysts that helped bring many people to Jesus and into the church. We saw so many people converted and their lives changed forever. The community was beginning to feel the impact of the Holy Spirit. At the same time, there was a great effort by the religious establishment to stop the move of God and silence us. They even made an unholy alliance with the demonic people who would come into our meetings just to discredit what God was doing in and through our lives.

Many of our family members were also persecuted because of our faith. The Catholic priest confronted my grandmother and rebuked her saying that she needed to get that grandson of hers out of that church right away. But nothing could stop what God was doing. There is no power in hell or on the earth or even in the realm of the principalities and powers that rule in heavenly places that could. (Eph. 6: 10-12; Mt. 16:18) The natural and the supernatural opposition was great but the powerful wind of the Holy Spirit that was blowing through the Mohawk Valley was greater. That same anointing that God had desired years earlier was now happening. Those who opposed us were everywhere, but we knew we had God. If God be for us, who can be against us?

I can honestly say we did nothing to hurt the church we left or any other church in the region that was serving God and preaching Jesus. We had one goal and that was to lift up the name of Jesus and bring all people to him. Miracle after miracle continued to show His favor and blessings over what we were doing, and they have continued to this very day. Home groups played an important role in growing the church. No one, even today, could minimize the importance of the brethren gathering together in homes to extend the arm of the church. People are touched on a personal level, make friends, gain prayer support and more.

During this time period, the Holy Spirit was moving in such a powerful way. Pastor Mingo's slogan was "If you can't have a revival, you might as well have a riot!" You may think that's radical but consider Acts 17: 4-6:

Some of the Jews who listened were persuaded and joined Pau and Silas, along with many God-fearing Greek men and quite a few prominent women. But some of the Jews were jealous, so they gathered some troublemakers from the marketplace to form a mob and start a riot. They attacked the home of Jason, searching for Paul and Silas so they could drag them out to the crowd. 6 Not finding them there, they dragged out Jason and some of the other believers instead and took them before the city council. "Paul and Silas have caused trouble all over the world," they shouted, "and now they are here disturbing our city, too. (NLT)

Further on in verse ten: "That very night the believers sent Paul and Silas to Berea. When they arrived there, they went to the Jewish synagogue." (NLT) It's clear in the Word that there were those who were ready to receive and those who were not. Scripture shows us that the religious leaders of the day were envious, plotting and hateful. The crowd was stirred into an uproar. The goal was to attack the house of Jason (v. 7), a believer and one who moved in healing, and drag him off to prison. Jason and other believers were the ones who stood against the establishment and turned their city upside down no matter the cost. (v. 6)

There will always be forerunners willing to pay the cost for the next move of God. That's what a true reformer is; our battle cry was 2 Cor.6:16-18: "And what union can there be between God's temple idols? For we are the temple of the living God. And God said: 'I will live in them and walk among them. I will be their God, and they will be my people.'" (NLT)

Andre Crouch's song "Through It All" was one of the songs in my heart during those days. When the enemy would try to bring confusion and disappointment or stop us from moving forward, we would lift up our voices in worship and praise, praying for His guidance. This song would capture that:

Through it all, I learned to trust in Jesus
I had many tears and sorrow's
questions about tomorrow
There were times where I did not know right from wrong
but in every situation
God gave blessed consolation
my trials come only to make me stronger
I thank God for the mountains and the valleys
and I thank Him for the storm. He brought us through
and if I never had a problem,
I would never know that He could solve them.
I would never know what faith in Him could do. Andre Crouch

Chapter 13

All Our Children

Will be Taught of the Lord

We are grateful and can never overstate the importance of the local church upon our family. The church provides direction, support, and encouragement that the world cannot offer. It goes beyond the activity level that many parents seek to keep their children occupied and please note, I'm not against wholesome activities or involvement outside the church. But I am committed to the undeniable power of the Word of God and the need many parents have for others who will come up alongside them and pray through situations and problems that will occur in every family. The Word of God and support from other believers is priceless. However, having said that, being the children of pastors can present its own set of challenges even within that safe framework. Rita and I really want to thank and honor our children for their love, encouragement, support, and their willingness to make the sacrifice that it took for us to be able to do what God called us to do. Thank you, Tommy, Toni, and Steve.

Each of our children with their spouses, Erica, Jon, and Magalitta, have given us the greatest treasure on this earth—our grandchildren Lileana, Fiona, Emmanuel, and Gioacchino (Rocky) We love you, Papa and Mema.

When Rita got pregnant with Tommy, it was a miracle! Due to a physical issue, Rita was unable to conceive. One day Brother Mingo had a word of knowledge concerning Rita's condition and called her forward and prayed for her to be healed. Within two months Rita was pregnant with Tommy. Fourteen months after Tommy was born, our beautiful daughter, Toni, was born. About that same time, prophet Bill Hamon came to minister at our church and as he was prophesying over Rita, he declared that Rita would have a healing ministry especially for couples who were barren. To God's glory, there are about 25 young people alive today because of that ministry of healing.

One couple had been married for 17 years. They tried everything that was available and were really at a point of hopelessness, but God! Rita had a word of knowledge for them that they would have a child. About a year later, they had a boy. A pastor's daughter from the Caribbean was having great trouble getting pregnant. Rita did not know anything about the situation. She prayed for the young couple that God would give them a double portion of their heart's desire. About a year later, they had twins. There are also several couples who were unable to have a child and sought Rita out for prayer. By the miracle-working hands of our Lord and Savior, they all received children.

From the moment that Rita and I knew she was pregnant, we began to pray for our children that we would have an understanding that no one is an accident and every person has a destiny.

Our prayer was: *Father God, In the name of Jesus, we pray that our children will never know a day outside of your camp. We pray that they would always serve and worship You and that their spouses would love You. Together they would cherish and love one another and serve you and that even their children's children would as well—even as many generations until you come back.*

In that time of prayer, God would begin to show us what the call on our children's lives was as well as their spouses. We also prayed we would have a good relationship with their in-laws and to the glory of God, we have an awesome relationship with all of them. They really became family to us. We love them all so much and thank God for them. In Ps.78:4-7 it states:

> We will not hide these truths from our children; we will tell the next generation about the glorious deeds of the Lord about his power and his mighty wonders. For he issued his laws to Jacob; he gave his instructions to Israel. He com manded our ancestors to teach them to their children so the next generation might know them even the children not yet born and they, in turn, will teach their own children. So each generation should set its hope anew on God, not forgetting his glorious miracles and obeying his commands. (NLT)

Too often we hear about generational curses but at the cross of Jesus Christ those curses are broken and we begin a new genera- tional blessing by the blood of Jesus Christ which blocks out the iniquities or sin of the fathers. No sin has power over us. The only time it gains power is when we step out of the shadow of the cross, out of the protection and covering of our Lord Jesus Christ. There is an old saying that God has no grandchildren. How true this is and everyone must come to the place of accepting Jesus as a personal savior; we all must come to that place where He is not only our God but becomes our God and Savior.

I would like to tell you that we never had a problem or struggle with our children and that everything was perfect and wonderful. Of course, you would know that wasn't true. From the beginning we determined to pray for our children and declare what God had promised us for each of them. No matter how dark or hard the circumstances became, we would never let go of the promise of God for their lives. You can always be certain that there will be challenges.

First Timothy 1:18 states, "This charge I commit unto thee, son Timothy, according to the prophecies which went before on thee, that thou by them mightest war a good warfare." (KJV) What a powerful Scripture when you realize you can take the Word of the Lord over your life and your children's and do warfare with it. Rita and I have done this for all three of our children in seasons that were very difficult, where it seemed like they were not heading in the direction of God. Miraculously, over and over we saw the course of their lives change to the purpose and call of God.

The parable of the prodigal son is so powerful and wonderful but it also could be called the parable of the unconditional love of the father. I will briefly share with you some of the testimonies in the lives of my children, but I also want you to understand that it's so important that we give our children that unconditional love; don't ever close the door to your heart or your home to your children no matter how dark or bad it might get. It doesn't mean you accept their lifestyle or their sin. Always keep that path open because if they don't feel they can come to you, they will find someone else and for sure, the devil will put others in their path to keep them bound. In the parable in Luke 15:17-19, we see the son's revelation:

> And when he came to himself, he said, How many hired servants of my father have bread enough and to spare, and I perish with hunger! I will arise and go to my father, and will say unto him, Father, I have sinned against heaven, and before thee, 19. And am no more worthy to be called thy son: make me as one of thy hired servants. (KJV)

It says the father saw him and did not wait for him to reach him first. The father ran and embraced the son, kissed him and made a celebration stating, "My son that was lost is now found!"

While watching Billy Graham's funeral, his youngest daughter tells the story of a time she had drifted far from her father's teachings. When she came to her senses, she turned and went home and when she got there, her father was standing outside waiting for her. As she got out of the car, he came running to embrace her. That's the unconditional love of the father. I read that in the Middle East old men did not run and the father running to the prodigal son is symbolic. (Williams, 2010) The neighbors would have known of this backsliding and of the sins of the younger son. As onlookers often do, they probably met him with judgment and condemnation. Perhaps in the story, the father runs to spare his son the harsh judgment of bystanders.

It's always amazing to me that self-righteous and sometimes hypocritical people are so quick to judge others, but at the moment the issue hits their home, they hide it or make excuses desiring the mercy they did not render. They expect everyone to be totally understanding, but that's not the reality; we are warned in Mt. 7:1 "Judge not, that ye be not judged." (KJV) Rita and I have always made it a priority to pour into ministers' children especially in seasons in their lives when they were becoming cold to the things of God or are backslidden. We will take them out for pizza or something. We share with them that there are a purpose and a plan for their life. We also share the love of God. Today many years later, they're in leadership serving God and we have the privilege of serving them. There was one man of God who did that for our Tommy, and we thank God so much for him and his wife. That was Pastor Dudley Mays and his wife, Winnie.

When our son Tommy was born, it was like he was the crown prince. There were over 100 people that came to the hospital to see him. He was born on July 10 on brother Mickey Mingo's birthday.

Brother Mingo took Tommy into his arms and lifted him up to the Lord and prayed. As he was praying, he began to prophesy over Tommy's life that he would have a double portion of his ministry and that God would use him in preaching, prophesying and healing the sick.

On another occasion, when Tommy was four, a prophet came to minister at our church. We had a Christian school and daycare at the time. After he finished the chapel service and was praying over all the children, he said that he still felt there were more children he wanted to pray for. I told him we had a nursery and he asked me to please bring them out. As the children from the nursery came into the sanctuary, the first one to be called out was our son, Tommy.

The prophetic word over Tommy started with *TOM*! That really got our attention because that's what we called him so he would learn how to spell his name. The prophet continued to say, "By the time you're 17 years old, you'll have a double portion of your father's pastoral calling; you will preach, prophesy, and lay hands on the sick." We were so proud of our little man of God!

By the time he reached 15 though, Tommy began to show signs of rebellion. At 16 it was in full gear. I prayed God would give him a job so that he had to work on Sundays. That way when the people asked, "Where is your son?" I could say that he had to work today.

As I mentioned earlier in I Timothy 1:18, his mother and I began to pray and declare, "God, You said that by 17 You were going

168

to touch him and he would be on fire for You." We continued to pray. Rita was so bold in her prayer that she would say month after month as time would go by, "You have 5 or 4 or 3 months down, Lord." (meaning time was passing until that point where he would be 17 and ministering as was prophesied) "You're not a man that you should lie."

I mentioned his birthday was July 10. On July 9, the day before his 17th birthday, we sent him to a Christian camp kicking and fighting all the way. He did not want to go. All the parents were waving goodbye to their kids. As they loaded the bus to pull away, Rita and I were standing there saying to the Lord, "God, you have one more day." About 6 PM that evening the youth leader who had come to do the camp called us. He said Pastor Fedele, "These are the most rebellious children we've ever had to work with," and he said, "By the way, your son, Tommy, is the worst!" That's just what every pastor wants to hear. As we hung up the phone, we began to lift up our voices in prayer and Rita said, "God, you have six hours."

It was 11:58 PM and all the lights were to be out and everyone went to bed but not in my son's room. There were several young men in the same rebellious path as my son. Earlier around 11pm that evening, they began to talk about their parents' faith—all this stuff about Jesus this and Jesus that. They began to say, "We just don't get it!" Tommy is very much like his mother. He looked up to heaven and said, "God, if you are really like our parents say, show us." As the clock struck midnight on July 10, Tommy's 17th birthday—not a day early or a day late— the power of the anointing of the living God began to fall upon on those boys in that room. They fell to their knees and began to cry and repent and speak in tongues. The staff and the youth pastor at first thought it was a riot. They ran to the room only to be slain in the Spirit themselves.

This was the start of the revival that went through the entire youth group, boys and girls, and it was on Tommy's 17th birthday! The youth leader in charge, who knew nothing about the prophecy over our son's life said, "Tommy, will you preach?" He preached and the youth minister said, "You have a prophetic word for me," and he prophesied over the youth leader, Pastor Jude. To this day he will declare that was a turning point in his life when God had spoken to issues he had put before the Lord. There were also healings that took place. Truly to God be the glory for the things He has done!

I would like to say that was the end of the story, but you must understand that you have to fight the good fight of faith and contend for the Word. The enemy of our soul does not want us to reach our potential.

For almost 2 years Tommy was on fire for the things of God leading many young people to the Lord. During this time, he attended one meeting where he was prophesied over by inexperienced ministry with no senior leadership present. The word he was given was that he would be like Nebuchadnezzar, eating grass in the woods and losing his mind. In another part of the book, I discuss word curses. I believe that's what happens when the enemy takes what was spoken and uses it as a curse.

Because we saw what it did to our son, we are very cautious. He received a prophecy on Saturday and on Sunday morning he walked up to me just before I had to go to the platform to preach and said, "Dad, I am getting the hell out of here. I've done everything I know to please God, but it's not good enough for Him, so I'm leaving." Tommy walked out of the church and that season of backsliding lasted five years.

Once again Rita and I began to declare, "God, You said do spiritual warfare through all those years; and sovereignly by the mercy of God, you set our son free. Now, at the point where he was getting right with God, the devil wanted to kill him. God, we believe you for the good plans you have for his life. We know you will finish the work you have started in him!"

The Lord is faithful and Tom returned and was restored. Shortly after, God began to work miracles in his life. They were so great; he would never be able to say that God did not love him. They were designed for him alone by an almighty God. One, in particular, occurred several months after Tommy got right with the Lord. He said to me he wanted to go to Bible school. Neither of us had the money and so it would have to be a real provision of God. Tommy's faith was very high. He began to look into several different Bible schools. It had been quite a while since he and I did

171

anything together and so I had heard that Rob Parsley's pastor's conference was quite powerful and he had a Bible school. I said to Tom, "You and I should go and you can check out the Bible school."

On the last day of the conference, Pastor Parsley said for the final offering that you must bring it up and lay it on the platform and believe God for that which is on your heart. Tommy turned to me and said that he was going to give his last $20 to believe to attend Bible school there. As we began to walk forward to put our offering on the platform, one of the ushers tapped me on the shoulder and said, "Brother, may I ask you what you're offering is for?" I said, "This is my son, Tommy Fedele. He is giving his last $20 to believe to be here in Bible school by December." At the time it was September. After a few minutes, the ushers returned and said, "Pastor Rod Parsley wants to see you both on the platform." I had never met Pastor Parsley nor did he know who we were. I persuaded Tom to go forward with me. When we got there, the head elder asked what our offering was for. I said, "This is my son, Tommy Fedele; he is giving his last $20 and believing to be here in Bible school by December."

Pastor Rod Parsley looked at Tommy as if his eyes were like an x-ray machine and said, "Who do we have here?" We were introduced and the elders explained what we were believing for. Pastor Parsley turned to the congregation of pastors and said, "I need two pastors who will pay a year each for this young man to come

172

to Bible school and, by the way, the cost is $10,000 a year. Within minutes two pledges were paid. Tommy graduated from Rod Parsley's school and has served the Lord in many different capacities.

He has a tremendous heart for soul winning. Today, he is a faithful husband, a loving father and a great son!

Our second child, Toni, was a very precious young girl and very gifted in drama and singing. In school from the time she was about 8 to 10 years old, there was a girl in her class who did everything in her power to make Toni's life miserable and she was succeeding. This girl found every opportunity to bully and torment our daughter by saying nobody wanted to be her friend. They all belonged to this girl's club and Toni couldn't be a member. Every day, she would come home crying. Rita spent a lot of time praying with her. She always told Toni every present is wrapped up very pretty on the outside but what really matters is the gift inside the box. Rita also reminded her that the Bible says you reap what you sow. She was told never to take things into her own hands and to let God deal with others and keep her heart right and clean. She also told her that everyone in life struggles. If you learn your lesson and act rightly before the Lord, you won't have to go around the same mountain over and over and over.

Time passed and then suddenly the Lord provided some very special gifts to us. Two new families came into the church. Keith and Tonette Noad came with their three children Erica, David, and Christie. Erica and Toni became quick friends and are still very close today. When that bully said to Erica, "If you're going to be Toni's friend, you can't be in my club" Erica said, "Then I guess I'm not going to be in your club. Toni and I are going to start our own club!" And they did! Soon after, most all the girls joined with Erica and Toni. The second family was George and Darlene Haggerty and especially their daughter, Cheryl who also became a great friend to both Toni and Erica. These families have been our lifelong and trusted friends; they've had our backs in prayer and demonstrate the importance and provision of the local church in walking out our lives as Christians.

In some ways, this can seem a simplistic situation but when your child is suffering and you can't change the circumstances, it is heart-wrenching. These times provide opportunities for life lessons but it isn't easy. Without faith and the Lord's guidance and direction, the middle school and high school years can be very challenging and key turning points in a young person's life.

Keith and Tonette became very close friends, really like family. They were there for me and my family over the years in so many ways. From the earliest days of our traveling ministry, they helped care for our children. We could never thank them enough for all they have done. Keith has gone home to be with the Lord and it has been a great loss to me personally as well as my entire family

As an aftermath, a couple of years ago Toni reached out to the girl who had bullied her in those early years and told her she forgave her for all the mean things she did to her as a child. She never heard back. Remember what I said about forgiveness? It's really for you because most often the person you're forgiving will deny they ever did anything wrong and they don't change. What changes is that you're no longer in the prison they created for you. It was the same with Joseph and his brothers in Gen.50:19-20. Today, Toni is a confident, powerful businesswoman, worship leader, devoted wife, a loving and caring mother and a daughter that any parent would be so proud of.

Steve was our surprise baby. He was born about six years after Toni. He was a miracle! When we first found out that Rita was pregnant, she was already three months along; after the administration of the ultrasound, the doctor told us there was a problem. The baby was going to be born mentally and physically handicapped and we only had a short amount of time for an abortion. Rita became very bold and told the doctor, "That is not an option for us. My Lord will give us the strength to face whatever challenge comes. We're going to pray and believe God for a miracle!" And that's exactly what we got. He was born perfect!

From the time Stevie was two years old, whenever he saw someone with any type of disability, he would want to pray for them. One day when he was about four, I brought him to gymnastics. I met a lady who was a good friend of my Aunt Ella. The woman had fallen and broken her shoulder bone. She was going to have surgery in the next few days. I was carrying him in my arms and he just reached out his little hand and laid it on this lady and said, "Be healed in Jesus name." The next day, my aunt called me and said, "What did Stevie do to Helen?" I said, "Nothing, why?" Ella explained that she went to the doctors and they told her she no longer needed the surgery. She said when Stevie prayed for her, she felt the heat in her shoulder and the pain was gone. The doctor didn't understand what happened but her shoulder bone was healed. Steve was an almost perfect child all through school until graduation, but after some bad decisions, he felt like he had no future. He was always dressed and groomed to perfection but due to some of those bad choices, his life began to unravel. He was already heading up the business ladder and was a great success. He had been hired by a Swiss company to represent them in America yet his life was spiraling downwards. He seemed to be losing everything.

Over a period of 10 months, he had reached a very low point. His brother and sister and Rita and I literally surrounded him. I began to pray, "You were not born for this. There's a call of God on your life. You have a purpose and a plan and there is a future for you. I break the spirit of oppression that has overtaken you." Through this whole ordeal a family heirloom was stolen from him. It was a ring that had belonged to his great grandfather; it was a black onyx with the gold letter F on it. The Lord spoke to me to buy him another ring and to put it on his finger. At the moment the ring went on his hand, we literally saw in the spirit as we were praying, four massive ropes, the type that usually tied a ship to the port,

176

come up out of his head and they disintegrated. The ropes represented the ties that were binding or oppressing him. Steve began to declare, "I want my life back, and I want my job back through those 10 months."

I never shared with him that his boss had said to me they know that Steve was the key part of their business and they would hire him back. At that very moment, the phone rang and it was his boss from Switzerland asking how Stevie was and that they wanted to hire him. His life began to climb to new heights. He rededicated his life to God and became a very strong man of God.

As this entire book proposes everyone has a destiny, we must seek the Lord and pray and He will lead. There was a beautiful young lady in France, Magalitta, originally from Sicily. When I saw her the first time, I declared that she would be my daughter-in-law. When she was eight years old, her mother told her that she would marry an American Italian but she must pray and write down what she wanted for her husband and this is what she wrote:

I want an Italian American man, about 6 feet tall. I would like him to be handsome, have black hair, and one dimple; I want him to be a hairdresser. I also want him to be in University for a higher degree.

Steve has a degree in cosmetology and also has an MBA in Strategic Management and International Business. And if that's not enough to convince you that God has a plan for your life, before Magalitta ever met Steve, she had been in several of our meetings in France and said to her friends, "I would like my husband and I to do a ministry like Stephen & Rita Fedele!"

Steve is a visionary and has a tremendous burden to help the poor. One of his future goals is to be successful enough in business that he could help missions and is now doing so through a branch of Prophetic Voice Ministries. He is a devoted, caring, supportive husband, father, and son.

In the life of each of our children, we had to take a stand and trust God. We declared the promises of God over their lives and with all fought the good fight and did spiritual warfare with the Word of God. If we do what is possible, the God of the impossible will work on our behalf, so pray and believe and stand on the promises of God. He will not fail you.

God's ways are perfect. The plans that He has for each of us are perfect. As we trust Him, we can be sure we are walking down the best path for us but also for all those we encounter. It's not just about one person. Though He loves us perfectly, it will always be about our destiny and how we affect others

Chapter 14

Upon the Solid Rock

As God continued to move, we began to see people with an anointing on their lives come from different regions and join us. At just that moment in time, several couples arrived who played key roles in what God was doing. Tom and Renee Burgess, Paul and Patty Schilling and someone who will always be close to our hearts, Bernice Schilling, who's with the Lord now. We thank God for each of them.

One of God's miracles of provision was to give us an old public school building which we turned into a church and a Christian school. There were even apartments for some of the young people. It was located in Ilion, New York. This was a village a short distance from Herkimer and Mohawk where we had started the earlier meetings. The Lord was truly moving throughout the valley.

At this point the initial church, which had grown from Joanne's home Bible study, began to multiply even more. Pastor Micky Mingo came on the scene. He was a man of God, mentor, friend and he was also an evangelist. I used to joke and say he started churches everywhere and anywhere like my grandmother's rose garden. She would walk in the yard, dig a hole with the heel of her shoe, and plant the rosebush with seemingly no rhyme or reason to it. Looking back at this now, I realize that Pastor Mingo was really a church planter. His evangelistic and prophetic anointing had the ability to draw a crowd very quickly and many people would be saved, healed, and delivered. A new church would be birthed out of these meetings but unfortunately at that time, there was no strong teaching on team ministry and particularly teaching about the Ephesians 4:11 or the Five-Fold Ministry for the equipping of the saints. Eph. 4:11-13 states:

> And He gave some as apostles, and some as prophets, and some as evangelists, and some as pastors and teachers, for the equipping of the saints for the work of service, to the building up of the body of Christ; until we all attain to the unity of the faith, and of the knowledge of the Son of God, to a mature man, to the measure of the stature which belongs to the full ness of Christ. (NASB)

The apostle, prophet, evangelist, pastor and teacher, are also referred to as the apostolic; when this word is used, it is referring to all five. The five-fold, or hand ministry, are the gifts or the offices the Lord gives to the church to build and prepare those who minister to the Body of Christ. He does this so His church would continue to grow and prosper. Because of the lack of understanding regarding these ministries and how they work in cooperation with one another, many of our branch churches did not go on to grow or have an impact in their community.

The Link of Eph. 4:11 to Our Destiny

At this time, Rita and I were sent out to pastor the church in Utica, New York. In those days, all our churches were called The Full Gospel Church of whatever the name of the village was where it was located. For us, it was our city, Utica, New York. Pastor Mingo had sent several couples to pastor that church who stayed about a year or so and left for various reasons. Out of desperation, Pastor Mingo then asked Rita and me to take the church. As I've said, there was no real understanding of the five-fold ministry of Ephesians 4:11, so teaching about this was critical. Training leaders and the congregation to understand the importance of this ministry became a priority for the fulfillment of Eph. 4:12 which says, " [and He did this] to fully equip and perfect the saints (God's people) for works of service, to build up the body of Christ [the church]." (AMP) At that time we were sent out with very little training but we had the sense that God was with us and we moved forward by His grace. The following comments are from my wife Rita, regarding the beginning of our pastoral ministry in Utica, New York.

From Rita:

When we were sent out into the ministry, taking over the Utica church, it was both an exciting and scary time. As my husband stated, we had very little training about local church order or the fivefold ministry. Our desire was to bless God's people and build His church. We threw ourselves on our knees in prayer and asked God for His wisdom and a revelation of His goodness and mercy. He downloaded by His spirit all that we needed. When the Lord spoke to us, we would put into practice what He had spoken. We saw firsthand how the church group and the people were blessed and established when we built according to His Biblical pattern. It

181

became so strong in our hearts and spirits, we knew that it had to be shared with all the churches to empower them to move in all the present day truth that Jesus had been restoring through the Holy Spirit.

Stephen was greatly used by the Lord to help pioneer the message of the local church government and order of the five-fold ministry with the apostle and prophet being foundational components, as it is stated in the Eph. 2:20. He has brought this to many churches, leaders, and nations, especially in Europe and the islands of the sea. God is always faithful to His Word and as we follow the Word, He will prosper it wherever it goes. (Prov. 16:20, ESV; Is. 55:11, KJV)

Thank you, Rita! Really, it's been a co-laboring together these last 45+ years. We had one true desire to help build the house of God which is the people of God. This is still burning in our hearts and we continue to bring these messages forward.

Rita and I understood what we had been commissioned to do and that was to share the gospel and see people get saved and established or planted in the house of the Lord. I shared earlier how important it is that we build strong local churches because that's what can make a difference in people's lives, strengthening the ability to have a successful walk with the Lord. Remember the theme of this book is everyone counts; everyone has a destiny and purpose—a role to fulfill the work of the Lord. Consider 1 Peter 2:5, "You yourselves like living stones are being built up as a spiritual house, to be a holy priesthood, to offer spiritual sacrifices acceptable to God through Jesus Christ." (ESV)

If there would be one thing for which we could be remembered, let it be that we were church builders and our desire was that the people of God would become all that God intended them to be, knowing no one is a mistake.

I have taught from the Scriptures for years that every church needs an apostle and prophet at its foundation. This Biblical truth must come to fulfillment; it is of the utmost importance for the next great move of God. Many times we've seen churches struggling to accomplish what they felt was their purpose. I believe real strength comes from the co-laboring of the five-fold gift ministries. (Eph. 4:11) Remember that hand imagery with five fingers? Each finger represents an office of operation and gifting of the apostle, prophet, evangelist, pastor, and teacher that can act with great power, strength and authority as they are functioning together. When we work in unity of spirit, that's when we are able to pull down the strongholds that come against individuals and the corporate church.

Apostolic offices are a representation of the full mantle of our Lord Jesus Christ while He was on the earth. As He ascended into heaven, He gave gifts to men. Eph. 4:8-16 explains these different mantles of authority which His followers would continue to use to build and lead the church. The Word declares in Eph. 5:26-27, "That he might sanctify and cleanse it with the washing of water by the word, That he might present it to himself a glorious church, not

183

having spot, or wrinkle, or any such thing; but that it should be holy and without blemish." (KJV) That's the goal—that His body, the church, be made ready for His return.

The church has much work to do. Apostle Paul tells us in 1 Corinthians 3:1-11 that he could not speak to them except as babes with the milk of the Word. They were carnal and not ready or mature to do what was needed. That's why the five-fold ministry was given as it states in Eph. 4:12—"For the perfecting of the saints, for the work of the ministry, for the edifying of the body of Christ."[21](KJV) Paul continues to instruct in 2 Timothy 1:13 and exhorts us, "to follow the pattern of sound words that you have heard from me, in the faith and love in Christ Jesus."[22] (ESV)

There are some wonderful nuggets of truth in 2 Corinthians 10: 3-5. It discusses building the foundation of the church according to the pattern in God's word which is critical. To paraphrase, we are not warring against flesh and blood. If we are going to pull down strongholds of the enemy, we have to walk in obedience to Christ. That's why every local church, every ministry, should have an apostle and the prophet at their foundation. We see that stated in Ephesians 2:19-21: Now, therefore, ye are no more strangers and foreigners, but fellow citizens with the saints, and of the household of God; And are built upon the foundation of the apostles and prophets, Jesus Christ himself being the chief cornerstone; In

---

[21] Strong's 3619 GR., building, like house builder
[22] Strong's 5198 Gr., not corrupt, healthy true in doctrine, 1319 teaching

whom all the building fitly framed together groweth unto a holy temple in the Lord. (KJV)" 1 Corinthians 3:3 reminds us, "For you are still carnal. For where there are envy, strife, and divisions among you, are you not carnal and behaving like mere men?" (NKJV)

As we continue to talk about the importance of having all the five-fold ministry influencing and touching our lives, as believers and as ministers of the gospel, it is also important that we understand no matter how anointed or gifted we may be, alone we will never be able to see the people of God come into their full ministry potential or service. In the equipping of the saints, it's important that they are exposed to all of the five-fold ministries. We must note that not every local church will have all five ministries in residence. In our churches, we may have one or two of them on campus but most churches will have to rely on traveling ministers, who carry the various gifts, offices and anointing, to come in to minister. The Spirit of the Lord is revealing this truth more and more. We begin to see a pattern of the Antioch and Jerusalem churches restored; the Word of God refers to the Antioch (Acts 13:1-2) or Jerusalem (Acts 15:2-4) churches. Not only did they have all the ministries represented, but they were also teaching and sending out ministry. When you are a leader or congregation member of an Antioch or Jerusalem type church, you're under the obligation by the Spirit of the Lord to share the resources of the ministries that are in residence. I

185

believe every trans-local minister must be connected to a local church and also to apostolic networks. No one should stand alone.

1 Thessalonians 5:12 admonishes us "to know them which labor among you." Every ministry and especially trans-local ministries must be accountable. We must always have checks and balances in our lives. It's not enough for someone to say they are sent of God. The most powerful Apostles, Peter and Paul, were also sent out by the authority of the church and had to go back and give a report. Remember, no one is an island unto themselves.

The Role of Spiritual Warfare

When we, or the corporate church, receive words of prophecy, we must test them (1John 4:1) and contend for those words. Scripture is clear that we are in a battle and it provides weapons and instruction on how we are to proceed. First, we need to take up these weapons and stand[23] on the offensive for war. Further, the Word of God is a living Word. In 2 Cor. 6:7 we are told how to go forth into the battle, "By the word of truth, by the power of God, by the armor of righteousness on the right hand and on the left." (KJV) The armor protects us on all sides and for every occasion. Consider each of the pieces (as described in Eph. 6:13-17) and what they reflect— the helmet, the breastplate, the sword of the spirit, the belt of truth and the shoes of peace. We are protected in every way by this armor.

---

[23] Strong's, 3695 to furnish, to be armed fully

Additionally, there are other tools. Remember, the Lord equips us; He gives us all we need. Some have referred to the image of eagles wings—one wing as praise and the other as prayer. These are two of the most powerful tools of spiritual warfare. When used effectively, Is. 40:31 tells us, "But they that wait upon the Lord shall renew their strength; they shall mount up with wings of eagles; they shall run, and not be weary, and they shall walk, and not faint."

Eph. 6:11a tells us to put on the whole armor of God; it is a picture of Jesus Christ who is the truth. Romans 13:14a: "Instead, clothe yourself with the presence of the Lord Jesus Christ. He is our righteousness and peace." (NLT)

His faithfulness makes possible our faith. He is our salvation and He is the Word of God so make yourself ready for battle by being fully armed in His armor and He will give the victory. I highly recommend a Bible study of Ephesians 6:13-17. Truly apply the armor of God to your life daily. Think of when King David pulled off his armor and returned to his palace. He was in greater danger there then when he was on the battlefield. Consider 2 Samuel 11:12 which says at that time of year when kings go out to war, David did not go to battle (or think of him as without armor); what followed? It was then that he was compromised when he pursued Bathsheba. We must realize we are never out of the reach of Satan's devices so we must never be without the whole armor of God.[24] The Apostolic career can be compared with a military career. This idea of the spiritual battle or spiritual warfare is not new.

Paul describes his encounters with trouble and difficulties in 2 Cor. 11:23-28. The apostle and prophet represent spiritual authority in the kingdom of Christ, almost as chief officers in the army. Remembering 2 Cor. 10:4: "For the weapons of our warfare are not carnal, but mighty through God to the pulling down of strong holds." This verse could read, "For the weapons of our apostolic authority are not carnal but mighty through God to the pulling down[25] of the strongholds."[24]

Think of a stronghold, in this instance, as something holding the mind and opinions or our imagination. I would describe it as a thought that impregnates the mind and emotions. I have spoken of my mother's mental illness from the trauma she suffered. I found this occurred with her. Once a thought was planted in her mind and took hold of her emotions, it became a reality to her. We are told that we must cast down imaginations in 2 Corinthians 10:5 and every high thing that exalteth itself against the knowledge of God, and bringing into captivity every thought to the obedience of Christ.[26](KJV)

---

[24] BE commentary NT

[25] Strong's 2506-2507 to lower, demolition of, destroy

[24] 3794 to fortify 2192 to hold

[26] Strong's 3053 referring to thoughts and reasoning

Once again we are being told that we're not to walk in the flesh or in a carnal way because we are not at war in the flesh but facing spiritual warfare. It tells us that our warfare is not fleshly so therefore we understand that it is spiritual warfare. You might ask, "What are we battling and how do we fight it?" In Eph. 6:11-12, we are told:

> Put on the whole armor of God, that ye may be able to stand against the wiles of the devil. For we wrestle not against flesh and blood, but against principalities, against powers, against the rulers of the darkness of this world, against spiritual wickedness in high places. (KJV)

Read those verses again and then go back to Eph. 2:2. It discusses, "the prince of the power of the air." Here is our enemy, the devil, and it follows in Eph. 6 10-17 with the kind of battle we are in and the type of armor to put on. We are told to take the whole armor of God in order to be able to stand in the evil day and here's our part—and having done all to stand. We are encouraged to be praying always with all power and supplication in the Spirit, and watching thereunto with all perseverance for all the saints; 1 Peter 1:13 says, "Wherefore gird up the loins of your mind" (be ready; have your mind focused); 1Cor. 2:1-5 (KJV) continues with how we should be prepared and be ready in our faith not standing on the wisdom of men but being dependent on the power of God. We are continually encouraged in the Word to remember our God and stand prepared in His Word. Isaiah 54:17a tells us, "No weapon that is formed against thee shall prosper." (KJV) We are in a war of the spirit. It is a real battle. A comparison Paul brings with the difficulties that oppose him in the discharging of his apostolic duty are as those of a soldier's warfare and pulling down of strongholds of the enemy.

This is why I teach that every local church and ministry must have an apostle and prophet at the foundation, working in cooperation with the pastor along with the evangelist and teacher, not lording over and wanting to be the ultimate authority, but with the Father's heart as a servant.

The Word of God puts these ministries at the foundation where the groundwork is done. One who serves in this capacity may not be seen as much as others, especially if they are not in residence, but it is undeniable they are a strong support to everything that is being built and are able to stand against the attack of the enemy. (2 Corinthian's 10:4, KJV) For the weapons of the apostolic—all five-fold ministry working together in cooperation and with authority—are not carnal but mighty to the pulling down of the strongholds.

I believe with all my heart that we will not see the next great move of God and resurrection of the dead as seen in Hebrews 6:1-2 until God has restored all the doctrines listed before the resurrection of the dead and when this has been completed, then comes the eternal judgment.

I want to state this very strongly—we will not see this take place until there is absolute cooperation among the apostolic ministries of Eph. 4:11. In our warfare, there are strongholds that must be pulled down. Those demonic forces in heavenly places (the prince of the air) will call for the full impact of the representation of Christ on the earth, the fivefold ministry, working together preparing the body of Christ to pull down and destroy the strongholds of the enemy and usher in the second coming.

As church builders our desire is to see the people of God become all that God intended them to be, knowing for sure that every one of us has a destiny and no one is a mistake. My prayer continues to be let us go unto perfection.

Chapter 15

Merging of Forces

The church grew. We sold the old building and bought a large factory in Whitesboro, NY which we converted into a church and Christian school. We changed the name to the Solid Rock Church. Once again, everyone in the congregation participated. By this time, Noel Howard and Jim Donnelly had come into the church from college. Noel had become a real craftsman and carpenter. He headed and directed the entire program leaving his full-time position to work on the building which could not have been done without the faithfulness of his wife, Debbie, who maintained their livelihood during the process.

For several months, the entire church would show up every Saturday for a workday. One day, Noel and some others were working on the roof where he had designed a bell tower. They were placing a cross on top when a young woman, Barbara, who was also part of our dance team, fell to the ground fracturing her pelvis. Her parents, who were unsaved, came immediately as she was hospitalized. Of course, there was such a negative tone over the whole event, but once again we saw God move. When she was released from the hospital, Barb came to church for Sunday morning service. The dance team had prepared a number in which Barb originally had a part. That morning as the anointing of the Lord filled the sanctuary, by faith Barbara began to step out and dance. She even leaped for joy and was miraculously and instantly healed. When she went to the doctors for a check-up, it was confirmed. Hallelujah! Thank you, Jesus!

At that time, we also began to develop a weekly TV show called, *Upon This Rock*. Just as we began to plan, Dr. Richard Raney and his wife, Leslie, joined us. He loved to work with video and had the equipment. The Lord provided at every turn.

So many more people were added that I wish I could mention each and every one of them but time does not permit. Without their strength and faithfulness to the vision that God had given us, we could not have accomplished all that was done in those early years. As the daily vision progressed, Rita and I could not help but notice something else. Every time a prophetic ministry would come to our church, the word over Rita and I was that God was going to send us to the nations of the world. If you remember earlier that was what the Lord spoke to me in the first two prophecies I received. Still, though, my heart was pastoring. I loved church, and I would resist the call until one time before a meeting, even before the prophets began to prophesy, the Lord spoke to my heart directly and said, "If you reject this call this time, I will never bring it back to you again." I knew right then, I had to yield to the will of the Lord. Rita was praying and asked the Lord to confirm it by Pastor Wilson asking us to travel with him. She prayed this for almost a year and at the very moment we needed the confirmation, Pastor

Wilson asked us to travel with him. It wasn't long after that he invited Rita and me to come to Holland to minister.

But my struggle was that I was a pastor of the church I loved. I felt that was my responsibility. How could I have this international ministry and still be pastoring the church? Then something happened. I was at a Larry Lee prayer conference with my friends, Mike and Barb Servello and Tom Burgess when the Lord spoke to me. There were thousands of pastors in the auditorium and we were worshiping the Lord. Suddenly, I had an out of body experience where I was hovering over the auditorium. The Lord asked me two questions. He repeated them three times. "Do you want My will to be done and do you want this kingdom to come?" As I answered yes to both questions, literally, I saw three buildings, the physical buildings of our churches. As each question was answered, the answer brought the buildings together so you could not know where one began and the other one ended. At that moment the Lord told me I would not be the senior pastor but Mike Servello would be. I was instrumental in Mike's conversion about eight years earlier when the Lord said to me, "I want you to hold his hands up and when the church is strengthened, then I will release you to the nations of the world." I thought, "How?" In two or three months, we would be gone but, of course, God knew what had to be done. Much had to be settled, both in my heart and in the work of the church.

We were not really full-time to the nations until 14 years later. Because this event took place away from home and it was so real and so powerful, I had already told Mike and Barb and Tom about it before I even spoke to Rita. She was my co- pastor; we have done everything together in the ministry from the very beginning so this was not only going to affect me but also her. When I got off the plane, I blurted out, "Rita, I've got to tell you something." She said, "I know! We're merging our churches together and Mike will be the senior pastor." Once again, the Holy Spirit had already spoken to Rita and settled it in her heart. I can't tell you what a blessing it is to have a wife so open to the things of the Spirit and willing to lay everything down over and over to do the will of the Lord. I would also include my children and my grandchildren who also have paid a big price for us to do what God is called us to do. I am so grateful to say that each one of them is serving God—truly to God be the glory!

The next challenge was to tell the members of our church what was happening. Of course, they would have to vote on this. I didn't want to make just one grand announcement from the platform so I started with the leadership team and the teachers of our Christian school. I went to their homes and told them what was happening and what God had told me to do. Every one of them, in total unity, agreed. When you bring three churches together, you have three sets of everything so there were obviously going to be those who were going to have to step down from their positions. Whatever was required of them, they did. Many times, we read about or know of church splits, but we broke that pattern when we brought these three churches together.

My new capacity was to be the elder overseeing, counseling, evangelism and of course, hospitality. Rita and I continued to do everything together. I was blessed that the church paid me full-time and allowed me one week a month to travel. That was a real blessing as we began our trips with mostly local ministry. There were a couple of times when I felt it was time to be released. Pastor Mike felt that it wasn't the time, so I submitted to his counsel. On one occasion, Sister Barb was very sick. She was a great support and blessing to her husband and the ministry and also has a prophetic anointing on her life. I had gone in to tell Mike that I wanted to be released and he said that he thought that perhaps he needed to step down for a while because of Barb's health. At that point, I said, "No. I will remain serving you as you continue leading the church. I will stand with you as you get through this season." When we began to pray intensely for Barb's healing, the Lord gave Rita a revelation of how to specifically pray for her and it was a turning point for Barb receiving that healing.

It was at that same moment in time that the Toronto blessing was occurring and people were traveling from all around the world to see and be touched by the Lord in this great outpouring. Mike and I, along with a couple of other people from our church, decided we would check it out. Many of the manifestations that were being reported were not new to us. Thirteen years earlier when Pastor

Mickey Mingo was having his revival meetings to start our church, most of what was being reported about manifestations, we had already experienced but we still felt compelled of the Lord to go. Our church had really grown and we were having powerful meetings. The church was full of faith for people and the worship was second to none. On the surface everything seemed perfect but there was something of desperateness on both of our spirits. We were hungry for something more. We had a notion that God was doing something new in the earth and we didn't want to miss it.

I talked about this earlier that periodically God brings a revival. While we were in Toronto, we witnessed so many different manifestations of people being blessed. Literally everywhere you turned, people were either slain in the Spirit, laughing uncontrollably or just groaning in the Spirit. But we left there seemingly with no impartation or outward manifestation. On the ride home, we discussed everything about the meetings and just called out to God. I said, "God, if You're moving in the earth once again, please do not pass us by; like Moses, if Your presence does not go before us, carry us not up hence." (Exodus, 33:15) That was on Saturday. Sunday morning we came into the church and everything seemed to be normal through the worship service. Pastor Mike got up to preach and with no warning was suddenly slain in the Spirit. Barb got up to try to handle the issue, and she was slain. I went up and the same thing happened. Next, like a mighty wind, the Holy Spirit blew through the whole congregation and many of the members were overcome by the Spirit of the Lord. In a moment, we were thrust into a six-month period of revival meetings. Every night of the week hundreds and hundreds of people came. We began to see people healed, delivered, and revitalized with a new passion for Christ in their lives.

It is important to mention here how vital it is to "pastor" revival—to keep a good balance of the preaching of the Word of God and the manifestations of the Spirit. I will say that Pastor Mike Servello guided the revival so well that our church was strengthened and through it, many ministries were birthed in the move of God. That's not always the case. We should long for the move of God and be open to the next truth that He's going to reveal to the body of Christ, but we always need to keep a balance. That's worth repeating.

It was noted that when we started our church, many of the religious establishment and people of our Mohawk Valley along with their pastors, who in the past had taken a stand against us, began to come. Even the church that we had to leave years earlier called and asked if they could come. Of course, we welcomed them. That entire congregation ended up coming and were in those meetings almost every night. A great healing and mending of hearts were done through the power of the Holy Spirit to where even to this day, there's a tremendous unity and cooperation among the churches in our area.

One of the things that came out of that revival was that Pastor Mike Servello was so impacted and so anointed, God began to move his ministry and the church out of the shadows into the light. At that time, we met Pastor Dick Iverson and Pastor Frank Damazio who were part of MFI (Ministers Fellowship International). This was a fellowship that helped connect pastors across the country and share resources. At the same time, Mike Servello had the vision to open up Compassion Coalition, which is a ministry where food, clothing, and personal products are obtained through donations and distributed to the poor. This ministry has expanded today nationally as well as to other countries around the world, especially when there is a crisis or natural disaster. Currently, there is a new 25,000 square foot building with plans for the future to expand to 40,000 square feet. Jesus tells us that the poor will always be among us and we believe you can never out-give the Lord. When you do something for someone who has nothing and cannot repay you, that's what really touches the heart of God. People asked how could your church's ministry be so impacting to your community and even beyond? The real truth from the very beginning—we were a people of generosity, always giving out and God honors that. The newly merged church was called Mount Zion Ministries.

A number of years later, the name was changed to Redeemer and is now under the direction of Pastor Michael Servello, Jr.[27] who

---

[27] Appendix A

continues to lead the church breaking every limitation that the enemy or man would try to set against the move of God. I'm praying for this next generation to arise and go further than we've ever gone and once again for the glory of God!

There is now the main campus in Utica, New York, and the overseeing Pastor is Michael Servello Jr. There are four satellite churches—one in Albany, another in Rome and a new campus in Syracuse, New York. If you ever read anything of Charles Finney's revivals, they actually took place along this route where we're located. Besides the Utica campus, there is also an International Campus welcoming the many refugees who come to this city. I believe God always had intended for the Mohawk Valley to be a hot spot for His anointing. I can only say what a privilege and an honor it has been to be a part and it's only the beginning. I can't wait to see what the Lord will do by 2027 when the ministry will be 50 years old. Without a doubt, we still will say *look what the Lord has done*!

Chapter 16

The International Ministry

Stepping into our international ministry was really a leap of faith. It was a part of the destiny God had planned for me tracing back to 1948 and that storekeeper's wife, Mrs. Mancuso, who had a word of knowledge from the Lord that she declared to my grandfather—"The child that's named after you will preach the gospel of my God!" She paused for a moment and turned back to him once again to say, "Unto the nations of the world."

The first two prophecies I ever received also declared that my name would be known throughout the whole earth. How would this ever become a reality, the poor backward boy who never left his village? The boy with a learning disability and insurmountable odds against him, but for God!

I thank God for my wife, Rita. She has an adventurous spirit and very little intimidates her. It was simple, if God said it, I believe it. I thought over and over, Who would ever bring us and how would we ever be able to step into an international ministry? It seemed impossible. In a time of prayer, the Lord told Rita that Pastor Wilson would invite us to go with him to Europe but the Lord also had told her not to say anything even to me. One day the Lord told her to tell me what she had been praying. No sooner did she finish telling me, the phone rang and it was Pastor Wilson. He said that he was coming over and to put on a pot for spaghetti. It was not unusual for him to stop by often as he had a home which was only about 25 minutes from where we lived at the time.

During that evening, he shared that he wanted to bring us to Europe. He went on to say that he believed our ministry would be greatly received and appreciated. He continued further that for the first five years, we would not be able to accept any meetings and we could only go where he brought us. We agreed to this believing it was a miracle provision from God. I also believed that Pastor Wilson and his wife, LouCelle, were the only ones who could have introduced us into an international ministry and this was the door we needed to be opened. There was much to learn and Pastor Wilson was the perfect teacher. It was such a privilege and honor to travel and learn from him and his wife.

It was 1993 and the first year we went with Pastor Wilson to a village in Holland that once was an island. Urk is amazing! Holland is the only country in the world that continues to grow geographically. They are geniuses when it comes to moving water and building dams. It's truly a wonder to see those huge dykes hovering over our heads, some a hundred feet or more with huge ships passing above.

The initial international meeting with Pastor Wilson was a conference and the very first people we met turned out to be the movers and shakers for the move of God in Holland. To this day, we are still very close with many of these men and women and many others, working in cooperation for the glory of the Lord!

We became close friends with Pastor Henk & Corrie Karelse, who have done our scheduling for Holland and Indonesia.[28] They, along with their daughter and son-in-law Pastor Michel and Sandy Van Zuthem, have hosted us in their home and transported us to many meetings for years. Without their help, love, and support, we would have never been able to accomplish what's been accomplished in the 25 years of ministry.

It still amazes me to look back over the years and see all the connections. How strategic and beautiful they are! At just the right time and from country to country, the Lord was and is there, and still today as we write, He is making connections.

Very soon after our first trip to Holland, supernaturally the Lord opened the doors to France and put a young pastor and his wife in our lives, Philippe & Marie-Louise Montuire. For almost 25 years, they have done the scheduling for France, Switzerland, and Africa. They also hosted us in their home and transported us to meetings for many years. We cherish their friendship, and they are truly a son and daughter in the faith. Pastor Philippe in his own right is a fantastic Bible teacher and preacher. It was through Philippe we met Apostle Michél Joéllé Marvane and countless other churches in France and Switzerland. Apostle Verner & Mado

---

[28] Appendix A

Lehmann and Evangelist Jean-Luc and Josie Trachsel of The International Healing Association, which is based in Switzerland, also became friends and contacts at this time. It was through our Holland ministry that the Caribbean opened to us. We met Pastor Arno & Loes Boetius of Aruba and from there we went on to Curacao and met Henk & Divina Boetiusa. Another very powerful and helpful woman was Mema Coco, who has since gone to be with the Lord. Her son, Pastor Ronald Coco, was also a help to us. Once again, it would be impossible to mention everyone by name but we love and thank you for your friendship and help.

For many of these churches, we serve on their apostolic boards and are recognized as a prophetic voice speaking into their personal lives as well as the ministry of the churches. This truly has been one of the highlights of our life and ministry.

I have often said this same thing of Dr. Eldon Wilson. He is really the Apostle of Presbytery, the 1Tim 4:14 ministry, sometimes called the laying on of hands. (Heb.6:1-3) He has brought this teaching and ministry to many nations of the world. Rita and I endeavor to continue bringing this message forward. We have also said that prophecy is one of the most misunderstood ministries in the Body of Christ today; that's why we started IPS—International Prophetic School and will add a mentoring program. It was a mandate from God for us to help raise up the next generation of prophets; along with that and very close to our heart is the apostolic ministry of Eph. 4:11, "And he gave some, apostles; and some, prophets; and some, evangelists; and some, pastors and teachers," (KJV) which we have pioneered through Europe by the grace of God.

Our apostolic and prophetic ministry has been recognized and received in many nations. We always align ourselves with the powerful apostolic ministry wherever we go and for the most part, it has been a wonderful experience. There have been a couple of times, though, we had to take a position defending the Word of God to both the pastors and leaders in some church complexes. I call it "The Blind Side of Ministry." In life, the truth is every man and woman of God will have a blind side at one time or another in their lives; that's why it's so important to always have checks and balances overseeing us, other mothers and fathers in the faith along with other apostolic ministry are the best choices so that we never stand alone.

What that provides is someone who can speak into our lives and bring insight or correction. We have lost some good friends because of this. It's not enough to just say that we submit or simply rely on another apostolic ministry to be that balance in our lives. There should actually be a written agreement so that all who are involved understand. We must truly exercise it, especially at times of great and crucial decisions for ourselves personally as well as in our ministry in the church and our family.

Over the years our ministry has grown to include mentoring the next generation of ministries, overseeing conflict resolutions, counseling and helping ministries through difficult situations, teaching in the Bible schools and pastor's conferences as well as working with many apostolic networks to help further their vision.

About 15 years ago, we had to make a decision that we would continue to build our European base or begin to establish a greater base here in the US, but we received such a strong mandate from God that Europe would be our main focus, we couldn't dismiss it. At the same time, we understood everything is tested. The Word instructs us in Deuteronomy 8:2, "And thou shalt remember all the way which the Lord thy God led thee these forty years in the wilderness."

Forty years—the number 40 is the number of testing, a new generation or new beginnings and it was the number of years God's people were in the wilderness.[29] I tell people all the time do not be afraid of the wilderness, the place of the test. You will come out successfully if you hold onto the Word of God and His promises which He has spoken over your life. Don't let it go no matter what you're facing and you will have success. That's what Joseph held onto. The test was to humble and to prove which means to test him, to know what was in his heart, whether he would keep God's commandments or not. (Deut. 8:2)

Once we made up our mind what God was saying to us and our heart and spirit aligned with the will of God, we were holding on

---

[29] Strong's, 3140

to His words. One of the biggest tests of our lives occurred when we were in France ministering. I became very sick out of nowhere. It was so bad that I didn't think I could even speak to minister. I got through the Saturday meeting only by the grace of God but through the night, things got worse and worse. On Sunday morning, I got up to minister. For 2 1/2 hours I preached, prophesied and prayed over many people and every symptom was gone. I thought hallelujah! I escaped whatever this was. But we soon found out that was not so.

When I was 16 years old, I was not saved. When my grandmother, my father's mother, was dying I was by her deathbed. She had been a practicing witch most of her life, and her death was the most horrifying death I've ever experienced, and I've been with many people saved and unsaved at their moment of passing. I made a mental note that I'd never wanted to die like that—with great fear, and I want to say that I did not feel fear that day in France when I became ill nor do I remember that day with fear.

We had to drive four hours to our next meeting. Our son in the faith, Pastor Philippe, was driving and I was in the passenger front seat. Rita was sitting behind me. Suddenly I was gone. I actually entered into heaven for the first time that day and before it would be all over, I would have died three times. That was March 15, 2009. Rita and Philippe realized that I was gone. Rita laid her hand on me and they both began to call upon the name of the Lord. First, I want to say it was through the prayer and perseverance of my wife and Pastor Philippe that helped me through this time and led to the amazing circumstances surrounding this miracle.

The following is Rita's account of that day:

I want to give thanks to the Lord and to Pastor Philippe Montuire who stood in faith with me taking authority in Christ to intercede and to call Stephen back from the dead. We were in the Normandy area of France. To begin, none of us were familiar with the area and we needed a hospital. The Lord sovereignly directed Philippe to the exact exit that we needed. As we exited, we saw the hospital sign. Glory to God!

When I began to call upon the name of the Lord, I was reminded of the first presbytery I ever received. It said that I would raise the dead! Never in million years did I think it would be my own husband.

I asked the Lord what I should do and asked Him to speak to me. I heard the audible voice of the Lord speak these words to me: "Every spirit is subject to the name of Jesus." It was so loud it soaked into every cell of my being. I said, "Okay, Lord! Tell me how to do this." The Lord said in an inaudible voice that I heard so clearly in my mind, "You must bind the spirit of infirmity, the spirit of death and the human spirit." I remember thinking that I didn't understand the last one but the Lord said it so clearly, I'm not going to take any chances. I'm going to do exactly what I feel He spoke to me. I spoke, "I bind you spirit of infirmity; I bind you spirit of death and in the name of Jesus I command you human spirit back" and Steven opened his eyes and took a breath. Stephen died one more time in the car, so I took authority again as the Lord directed. Once again, he took a breath and opened his eyes.

The third time he died was just as they got him on the stretcher at the emergency room. The doctor came out and told me they had resuscitated him but they had to put him on dialysis. They said if he makes it through the night, he will be on dialysis for up to 3 months or forever.

I felt faith once again arise and told the doctor, "No, Jesus did not heal him to let him live on a machine. My Lord is the great healer and you will see the power of God in my husband's life." Sure enough, we found Stephen the next morning off the dialysis machine with a clean bill of health. Two days later during my prayer time, I was thanking the Lord and He led me to Ps. 118:5: "Out of my distress I called on the Lord; the Lord answered me and set me in a broad place." A broad place means a large place, one of authority. In my lack of ability and in my distress, my weakness, Christ is strong and able. He will cause us to do all things as it states in Philippians 4:13 "I can do all things through Him who strengthens me." Even raise the dead!

This was a unique experience for me. When Rita called me back the first time, I had entered into this tunnel of lights but the lights were joy, peace, and love. I was going into this wonderful atmosphere of the love of God. As I was walking through the tunnel heading towards the source of all the light and the throne of grace,

I came to what I described as a sheer curtain and on the other side where silhouettes of people coming from different avenues seemingly celebrating something.

As I was standing just at the entrance of the sheer curtain, two thought's came to me—one was *if you go any further, you can't go back.* The second thought was *these are the jewels that will be in your crown that you will cast at my feet.* I instantly understood these were people who, in some way, I shared the gospel or the love of Jesus with and they had already gone to heaven. They are that great cloud of witnesses that Hebrews gives an account. We have to walk through them to approach the throne. It was exactly at that moment that I would hear Rita's voice each time commanding me to come back. She would say, "Steven, I command you in the name of Jesus come back." It was at that moment that I recognized three people and they were my mother, my mother-in-law, and my brother-in-law, Tommy, who had died about five years earlier.

When I talked about destiny and God's grace and love, I mentioned how Tommy was probably one of the main tormentors of our faith and the way we were bringing up our children in the Lord. He lived in California so we didn't have to put up with him much but when he was around, it really was miserable so much so that the man of God (me) said, "I will never witness to him again; it'll be a cold day in hell." All I can say is thank God we're not God!

For about 15 years whenever he was around, I avoided him as much as possible and then the phone call came; it was Tom. He told his sister that he was in fourth stage cancer and they didn't give him long. Of course, suddenly the mercy and grace of God's compassion fell on us and Rita made immediate plans to leave for California to pray for him.

When Rita arrived at the hospital, she told him she came to pray for him for healing but the most important thing is that he accepts Jesus as his Savior. Amazingly, he said he knew she would come for this and said, "Sis, I'm ready to accept Jesus." He prayed the sinner's prayer and she prayed for healing but in God's sovereign will, he was gone within 72 hours, though not before telling Rita, "Sis, I'm at peace and I know where I'm going. I want to thank you and Steven for always living your faith and sharing that with others. I know I gave you guys a hard time but I believe in Jesus." How good is God? 72 hours! He really didn't have a chance to live out his faith but he declared it and God accepted him and he was there—but for the grace of God.

I learned a valuable lesson that I continue to pass on; there's only one guarantee in this life and that is while we have breath, there's hope. There's no guarantee we will have it in the next moment. The Word of God says our life is like a vapor; it's here and then it's gone. Believe me, I know how true this is. We must live our lives to the fullest, every day, for His glory.

The fear of dying without being able to breathe stayed with me even through the years of my salvation, even as a pastor whenever I got a lung infection or some type of difficulty breathing. Fear would rise up in me. When Rita called me back the first time, the beautiful light and glory of the Lord were still with me and I remember sitting in the car thinking I can't breathe, but there was absolutely no fear and then suddenly I was gone again.

The second time Rita called me back, instead of saying, "Thank you, Darling! I said to her, "Leave me alone!" You see, I had absolutely no desire to come back. When I told this part of the story to my children, my daughter, Toni, was very upset. She said, "Daddy, your first granddaughter, Lileana, was just born; weren't you going to miss her and us?" I explained it this way, "When you're facing the glory of the living God and all His splendor and wonder, how could you possibly be looking back? You only have eyes for Him."

The third time Philippe actually found an exit that led to a hospital and as we were pulling into the emergency room entrance, I got out of the car, which I was so thankful for because French cars can be very small, and I thought, *Thank you!* I had gotten out! They'd have to use a can opener to get me out otherwise. But as soon as I stood up out of the car, the next thing I knew, my body was on the ground and my spirit was hovering over it. I was seeing everything from above. I saw Philippe running into the emergency room and the emergency room staff coming out with a gurney putting me on it and rushing me into the hospital.

What an amazingly strong and powerful wife I have! Rita was calm and in control. She walked into the intensive care room where

214

they were working on me and suddenly they heard a woman saying, "He shall not die but he shall live in the name of Jesus! 'Steven, I call you back in Jesus' name.'" One nurse said, "I think it's his wife." One doctor said, "Give her a sedative and get her out of here!" Rita put her finger, a prophetic finger, and said, "Don't you dare come near me. My husband is not going to die in Jesus' name." They escorted her out of the room. It was at that moment that everything went black. I believe it was the moment my spirit came back into my body.

It was about three in the afternoon when suddenly they sent a message to Rita that they had gotten a pulse. They warned her that she was not to get her hopes up because of the number of times that I had died and length that I was gone. They thought for sure I would have brain damage as well as heart and lung damage. They told her they had to put me on dialysis and said the next 48 hours will be crucial. Rita began to pray and said, "God, you did not spare his life to leave him on a dialysis machine, so I know that You're going to touch him and heal him in Jesus' name."

I woke up at about 7 PM. They just finished the procedure of putting the dialysis machine on me and the doctor came over looking at me very intensely. He said, "We have you somewhat stable. Don't try to talk; just rest." Rita and Philippe prayed and had to leave the area. I was alone and was unable to speak because of the breathing tube down my throat, but I laid there quietly and in peace.

I know it sounds silly but it was like I was on the beach just relaxing and this was all happening to someone else. I was at peace.

Suddenly about 1 AM in the morning, all the machines that I was hooked up to began to make some type of an alarm. Several medical people came rushing into the room. I think it's sort of what happens when someone dies and they're on these machines because one of the nurses noticed that I was watching everything and following them around the room with my eyes. She came in and looked very closely at me. I tried to smile. She went to the doctor, said something and he came over and got very close to my face. He looked at me for a moment and then turned back to the business of the room.

About 45 minutes later, they had actually taken the entire dialysis machine off of me and removed the breathing tubes. The doctor came to my side once again, took my hand and said, "All I can say to you is it wasn't your time!" Over the course of the next couple of days, we had so many opportunities for sharing the gospel. Some people even got saved and many of them were touched by the power of the living God.

Once again I would love to tell you that was the end of the story but of course it wasn't because everything gets tested. The doctors decided they would keep me in for one more day and they would release me on Tuesday. They said I would have to have an airline ticket to fly home immediately because the only thing they could come up with was it was my medicine that had caused this to happen. By the way, the physical, natural thing that was taking place in my body was both my kidneys had completely stopped. When that happens, you're going to go into cardiac arrest.

On Monday the chief administrator of the hospital stopped in; during this time, numerous people would walk by and just stop at the door and look in. As family members of other patients heard, they would actually come to the door and ask for prayer for their loved ones. Rita and Philippe prayed for several people during that day. Nurses would take blood samples for further tests. They were checking the amount of oxygen in my blood. As they were writing on my chart, I heard them speaking in French. I don't know French, but I understood what they were saying to each other that the oxygen in my blood was very low. A fear began to spring up in my heart. I immediately began to pray against the spirit of fear that I received when I was 16 years old, binding it in the name of Jesus. That night Rita was in her hotel room and a demonic voice said, "Steve will not leave the hospital!" At the same time in Philippe's room, a mocking voice said, "Steve is getting out of the hospital tomorrow in an undertaker's bag!"

It was just about 1 AM in the morning, exactly 24 hours after the Lord had healed me when something dark, so dark, came to my room and was in the doorway. I don't know if it was an angel of death or what but as it entered the room, the darkness filled it and something like a cape or wings swallowed the whole room. It covered my mouth and nose to where my breathing became very

217

difficult. The whole room was darkness. That horrible fear sprang up that I felt at my grandmother's death.

But I'm happy to report that spirit of fear was broken. I got out of the hospital and we flew back to the United States. Under the orders of the doctors from France, I had called my doctor at home even before I left Europe to set up an appointment. Of course, I was so excited about sharing a little bit of what had happened. The US doctor happened to be a Christian but I was surprised at the hesitation and negativity I felt from him about my story. I explained to the office that the French doctors told me not to take any of my medication until I would be checked out by the US doctors. Believe it or not, he couldn't see me for two weeks so, during that time, I was not taking my high blood pressure medicine or diabetic pills, which I had been on for years. I was taking 3500 mg of diabetic pills a day.

Though these miraculous events came to pass in Europe, they had their reach into every area of our lives and continued when we returned home. During the course of that unforgettable day when I died three times, a number of things were happening at home. Pastor Michael Servello had called us for emergency prayer for his son, Joey, who was being rushed to the hospital. At that moment Rita told him I had passed away; Michael and Barb were in such shock and facing their own crisis with their son. Of course, they began to pray as well as my daughter, Toni, who happened to call at that same time. She also received the same message and immediately called my sister, Pat, and Aunt Ella. When my aunt heard the news, she had a heart attack and was rushed to the hospital in very critical condition.

Once again destiny was coming to pass. I had promised my grandmother I would always be there for Ella and my heart was that she would not be alone at the time of her death. Now, how would that be possible? Understand, we were quite often gone so the chances of me really being by her side at the time of her passing were very slim, but for God! In the middle of all that was happening, Rita had the presence of mind to pray for Joey Servello and the Lord gave her a word of knowledge of what was wrong with him and sure enough, it was the word of the Lord. Everyone was praying and God be praised, Joey recovered.

When I came home, I had a number of medical appointments but decided I was not sitting around waiting for them. I knew I must go to my aunt's side and flew to New York. My aunt recovered and got out of the hospital. We had about a week and a half of such good times together thanking God for His goodness to us. In the middle of all this, my son, Tommy, was getting married so once my aunt was back on her feet and the wedding was over, I went back to Florida.

It was time for my doctor's appointment. He seemed quite doubtful even though I had all the medical records with me and said he wanted to do an MRI. I agreed. After my test, he called me within a day. He said he needed to see me in his office as soon as possible. We knew it was not going to be good news. The doctor told us there was a spot on my right kidney that didn't look good. He went on to tell me he wanted to do a biopsy. That same anointing and authority that came over Rita in the doctor's office years earlier when we were told that our son, Stephen, would be born handicapped, now seemed to rise up in me. At that moment I said, "I absolutely refuse to accept this report. Take another MRI." He scheduled it and sure enough, the test came back normal—there was nothing on my kidney.

That's another lesson I had to learn. The enemy will always try to rob your victory and sometimes he'll even use people to discourage you, but you must stand in faith unwavering like David. When his child was sick and dying, he fasted and prayed for a miracle for the Lord's healing power. When the child died, David did not get bitter but he refreshed himself and went back and worshiped the Lord. Sometimes things don't work out the way we hope or pray. One thing is sure, and we must always remember as born again Christians that our lives are in the hands of the Lord. No demons of hell or sickness can take our life if it's in the hands of God and God alone.

Another miracle that took place was financial and made it possible for me to insist on another MRI. They're quite expensive about $5000 and we had no medical insurance, but for the providence of God! One year before this event, my credit card company called me and said we were not taking full of advantage of all the benefits of our card. I asked what benefits I was not taking advantage of. They said, "For $149.00 a year, you and your wife can have $100,000 in emergency medical insurance." Believe it or not, I told them to let me think about it. Thank God, I called them back and enrolled in the medical plan. There were guidelines that you had to follow to be eligible and yes we met all regulations. When these events occurred with my health, it cost us absolutely nothing. It was about $40,000 by the time it was all over. Isn't God wonderful? He is the Prince of Peace.

Soon after, I received a phone call that my aunt was back in the hospital and it did not look good. I immediately returned to be by her side. I didn't let anyone know I was back in town, not even the church people. While I was at the hospital the first day, they had to do some work on my aunt and asked me to go to the waiting room. As I walked into the waiting room, I saw there was a large crowd of people holding hands and praying. I walked further into the room again and noticed these are people from my church. A sister came out of the crowd and said to me, "Pastor Fedele! You're here to pray for my husband." He had been in a serious car accident and had been in a coma for several days. She said, "What God did for you, He's going to do for my husband." She took my hand and led me through the intensive care unit of Saint Elizabeth's hospital in Utica, New York declaring at the top of her voice, "He was dead, but he's alive and he's going to pray for my husband, and my husband will live also!" Her husband happened to be in the next room to my aunt's. I stood at the foot of his bed; he was hooked up to all the machines as well and unconscious. I had just had this great miracle in my life. As I stood there I thought *I better do my best pastor's prayer.* Ye of little faith. Can you believe it? After what God had done for me! When I was about to say my prayer, I felt the unction and the power of the Holy Spirit say, "You're standing in resurrection power." So I did what Rita did. His name was Don. I said, "Don, in the name of Jesus, I command you to rise up now in Jesus' name." Absolutely nothing happened but I felt the authority in the power of the resurrection, an authority that caused me once again to say, "In the name of Jesus, Don rise up!" I remembered something Sister Wine once said when she raised someone from the dead in India. She noted that it was on the third command and so once again I said, "In the name of Jesus, Don, rise up," and he did! I want to tell you the truth. I believe it was the faith of his wife that caused that miracle because I was "ye of little faith." Don walked out of the hospital and lived for several more years. What an awesome God we have!

Within an hour the doctors had told my cousin, Cynthia and I that there was no hope for my aunt. In fact, she was in much pain even though she was in a coma. So we gave the order to take her off life support. Not only was I by her side, but also several other members of my family were there. How good God is! She was not alone but surrounded by loved ones.

Following these events, my children, my dear friends, and others from my family began to say, "How long are you going to keep doing this traveling ministry? You need to stop and just stay home!" I said to them, "If God did not raise me off that deathbed and heal my body and take me off that dialysis machine, I would've had no choice. I would've had to stop, but He healed me and raised me up!" So when will I stop? I will do this as long as He gives me the grace to do it. I will continue and once His grace is lifted, none of us can do more.

What God has called us to do, we can do. That's why Paul said in 2 Cor. 12:7-9:

> And lest I should be exalted above measure through the abundance of the revelations, there was given to me a thorn in the flesh, the messenger of Satan to buffet me, lest I should be exalted above measure. For this thing, I besought the Lord thrice, that it might depart from me. he said unto me, My grace is sufficient for thee: for my strength is made perfect in weakness. Most gladly therefore will I rather glory in my infirmities, that the power of Christ may rest upon me. (KJV)

We have seen so many miracles over the years! As we celebrate 25 years of trans-local ministry, 45 years of full-time ministry and marriage, and after 10 years since being raised from the dead, all I can say once again:

> *How can I say thanks for all the things You have done for me?*
> *Things so undeserved yet You gave to prove Your love for me.*
> *The voices of a million angels could never express my gratitude. All that I am and ever hope to be, I owe it all to thee.*
> ("The Tribute" Crouch, A)

So often people have asked, "What is the secret of the success and longevity of your trans-local ministry into Europe?" When we first started, we determined we really came to serve them and strove to demonstrate the words of Jesus in Mark 10:43b – 45:

> ...but whosoever will be great among you, shall be your minister: And whosoever of you will be the chiefest, shall be servant of all. For even the Son of man came not to be ministered unto, but to minister, and to give his life a ransom for many." (KJV)

The first seven years was a time of proving for us. People really examined and watched our motivations to see what we were truly about. Throughout these 25 years that Rita I have been coming to Europe, there was only one time a pastor paid for our tickets. All the other times, we paid our own expenses and never made a demand or told them what we expected in return. In the last couple of years, we've had to ask for some adjustment because the cost of transportation really reached a great expense.

In all this, we must say "To God be the glory!" We must be careful whenever God is restoring the truth to the church and striving to bring it into the balance. At one point in particular with the apostles and prophets, the pendulum swung completely to the idea that only through pastors, teachers, and evangelists would God restore the truth of the apostolic prophecies, but now that pendulum is swinging to the opposite side where some are asking for absolute authority with no checks or balances. What we truly need is that this truth would come into balance where there would be a great cooperation among the apostle, prophet, evangelist, pastor, and teacher working together, honoring and preferring one another, for the good of the body of Christ, the Church of Jesus Christ, Our Lord and Savior.

When it's out of balance, it's because we don't fully understand the Father's heart who sent Jesus who explained when you see me, you will see the one who sent me. (John 14:9) It will not be about what you can do for me but rather how can I serve you and your church? At that point, we will stop debating who is the greatest but rather seek a servant's heart and not look for the highest rank or desire pre-eminence. It will be those know the truth and display what Jesus taught his disciples who will see the true restoration of the apostles and prophets which are foundational ministries.

Think about it. Where do we find the foundation in a building? On the top of the steeple or in a brilliant star which says, "See me!" Is it not in the root which is deep in the foundation where the hard work is done and not always visible to all? It's where our hands get dirty doing the real building and strengthening of the work of God. We must understand it's not about lording over but lifting up the true Lord, the King of Kings, the Lord Jesus Christ. Our goal is that all might see He is the bright and morning star. Because we've been traveling abroad for 25 years, we have a view with the prophetic advantage of what God has done especially in Holland and other nations.

When we first came, we found pastors struggling to build good foundations for the local churches. Helping the local church has always been our heart and still is. We immediately came up along-side them to encourage the work of God and see it grow. We then targeted the raising up of team ministries and saw great progress in that area. Next, there was a move of God among young people. For nearly a generation, the things of God and the truth of Jesus Christ had been ignored and put away. Many of these young people had grown up knowing nothing about Jesus Christ other than His name as a curse word. They began to have powerful encounters with the King of Kings and the Savior of the world which changed them forever and helped to ignite a move of God in their nations.

In the churches over the last 10 years, we started to see the fruit of our labor and teaching of the five-fold ministry. Now I'm glad to report in all of the nations with whom we are presently involved, there are strong apostolic networks of pastors and church leaders truly moving in the things of God. Rita and I had the great honor of serving many of these on their apostolic boards. In Holland, in just the last three years, we have seen major ministry fellowships, though different and distinct in their call of God, coming into the unity of relationship to work together wherever possible for the good of the nation, the church and the kingdom of God.

In the last 10 years after the Lord allowed me to come back from the dead, I felt He put a mandate on my heart to help raise the next generation of the Eph. 4:11 ministries. By the grace of God, that's what we're doing with the cooperation of many of these apostolic networks and local churches.

Again I state, a true apostolic ministry for the 21st-century will not be about who can be the greatest in the kingdom but who can serve the most. Paul tells the Corinthians in 2 Cor 10:1 that spiritual power is in uniqueness and gentleness not in throwing your weight around. He uses his name, Paul, which was significant. Paul's name means little or humble[30] and interestingly he, (Paul), cautions all that a rise in position about how dangerous that positional power can be. It can be particularly dangerous for some who want to be preeminent, such as the chief rulers who in their quest to be at the top required everyone's submission and obedience; yet, they themselves refuse to be in submission. They don't want anyone to speak into their lives nor do they want to be in submission to anyone. No one is an island unto themselves; everyone must submit to someone.

Remember, if we get to a place where we think we have all authority—that's when there could be a great downfall. Your life, your family, your ministry and the testimony of the Lord could suffer. We need to always, as it states in 2 Cor. 10:5, practice "Casting down imaginations, and every high thing that exalteth itself against the knowledge of God, and bringing into captivity every thought to the obedience of Christ." (KJV)

Mark 9 33-45 also helps to clarify this. Jesus came to Capernaum a place whose name means of comfort.[31] It was a city that

---

[30] BE Commentary, BibleGateway
[31] Hitchcock's Bible Names

was flourishing. Like Esther who had finally reached a place of comfort, the Lord brings us to our place of destiny and as it was said to her, "...and who knoweth whether thou art come to the kingdom for such a time as this?" She was determined to follow God and pursue her destiny. (Esther 4:14, KJV) She sought God and came to the conclusion, "...and if I perish, I perish." (Esther 4:16, KJV) In other words, whatever the cost, I will humble myself to do the will of God. In these verses in Mark 9:33-35, it states:

> And they came to Capernaum. And when he was in the house he asked them, "What were you discussing on the way?" But they kept silent, for on the way they had argued with on another about who was the greatest. And he sat down and called the twelve. And he said to them, "If anyone would be first, he must be last of all and servant of all." (KJV)

Jesus, we pray that you would keep watch over our lives, all of us, as it is possible even the very elect can be deceived.

Conclusion

My prayer as you've read this book is that you would come to the understanding that God has a destiny for you through every stage of your life no matter the season, whether good times or bad. As we surrender to the Lord, He's able to take the pieces and put them together for a vessel used for His purpose and glory.

For our part, we need to continue to stay focused on the Lord so that whatever we do may benefit others. Our motivation should always be to please the Lord. Sometimes in life, there will come disappointment and discouragement even from the household of faith which is most difficult to endure. Like Joseph, never give up the dream that will bring you to your destiny, knowing with confidence that God hears your cry and will answer.

It's also so important that we always maintain a servant's heart no matter what God calls us to. The one thing I have come to rely on is that God knows what He's doing. I will always be thankful for the people He's put in my life. I must honestly say, *I thank God for the mountains and I thank Him for the valleys for if I never had a problem, I wouldn't know that He could solve them.* (Andre Crouch) I've come to depend on His holy Word.

In my early life, I had very little hope or expectancy to ever get out of that vicious circle in which I found myself. As I was writing this book, it has been reinforced in my heart and spirit over and over that God has a purpose for us, but we must choose not to live in the past or blame others. If we're always looking back and blaming someone else, we will never move forward. We must continue to be willing to listen and change from glory to glory. (2 Cor. 3:18) The only one who doesn't change is Lord Jesus Himself who is the same yesterday, today and forevermore. (Heb. 13:8)

Almost 50 years have passed from when I first called on the name of Jesus and as I consider what He had to work within me, I can say, "Truly, truly, if God can do it for me, He can do it for you. Lord, if you can use anything, you can use me!"

It's still all about that original creation story in Genesis 1:1-2.

Please look at this verse as your life before the Lord. When the Spirit of God moves over our lives, anything is possible. The Word tells us "In the beginning, God created the heavens and the earth." The earth, your life—"It was without form (empty) and void; darkness was over the deep." (v. 2) Liken this to the mass of waters. In Is. 43: 2 the Lord tells us, "When you pass through the waters, I will be with you; and through the rivers, they shall not overwhelm you." God has taken us and formed us. He is with us through all the challenges that confront us and He will hold onto us for His purpose and glory. Have you considered the path of your life? It's never too late to respond to His lead or promptings.

In 1Cor. 1:26-31, we are told He uses the foolish things to confound the wise. I don't know how you feel about your life but this really describes where I was when God found me or better yet when I found Him. The Scripture is so descriptive of all of us. Thank you,

Jesus, for your great power. We give you all the glory, honor and praise! Because of Him, we are in Christ. Jesus became to us wisdom from God, righteousness, sanctification, and redemption, so that, as it is written in Jer. 9:24, "Let the one who boasts, boast in this alone." It continues stating that God understands and knows me. (NASB) Think about that. God knows you. He understands.

From the bottom of my heart, I pray God's richest and greatest blessings upon your life and that you will step into all that God has for you. You can declare, as many have declared, I know I have a destiny.

Much love and blessings,

Pastor Stephen Fedele

Appendix A

Pastoral Testimonials

A Word from Pastor Michael Servello. Jr.

I have had the privilege of knowing the Fedeles for close to 40 years of my life. Probably the most significant moment for me regarding their ministry is a key moment when I was 14 years old. I walked down to an altar call Brother Fedele had given during a guest speaking appearance at our church in Herkimer, NY. That moment would mark a turning point in my life. Later that year our churches would merge, and I would have the blessing of being part of the Fedele's ministry for many years.

Through the years I have witnessed that the only thing that has matched their extraordinary gifting is their extraordinary love for people. You will not find a couple who love people more than the Fedeles. Their prophetic gifting is amazing! Honestly, I always thought they were amazing, but I really didn't see the magnitude of their gift until they returned to minister a few years after relocating to Florida. When they returned, I was blown away by the jaw-dropping accuracy of their prophetic word which was always ministered in a pastoral, compassionate way that makes you feel the heart of God. I could confidently say, along with my entire congregation, that every time the Fedeles are in the house, we are strengthened and built up!

It is a great blessing that God has allowed them to be part of our church family. The older I get the more I realize how blessed I have been, and I am convicted by how much I have taken such valuable gifts for granted. We don't often think about the environment we have grown up in and really just how much that environment has influenced our lives. I'm thankful that the Fedeles have modeled stability, love, character, and passion for Jesus to me, and so many others that they have touched through the years. They have served faithfully for 40 years and we know the best is yet to come!

Pastor Michael Servello Jr.

A Word from Pastor Henk and Corrie commenting on

our relationship and the teamwork

From 1998 till now the Fedeles have ministered in "De Banier" several times each year and we have been tremendously blessed by their ministry. Often they would stay in our home and at times we traveled together to minister in other countries, but we have seen what they are in private and what they are in public: ministers with a *good* report.

Their preaching and teaching are biblically sound, and their prophetic ministry is Spirit-inspired and very accurate. Through the years, countless people in our church and many other churches we are in a relationship with, have been blessed and strengthened in their walk with God because of the prophetic words they received through the Fedeles.

Many pastor friends have received wisdom and insight through their counsel, feeling very safe because they know the Fedeles honor the office of the Pastor. They will not prophesy over people when there is no leadership present to judge the prophetic word. We especially value their ministry in "presbytery meetings," many times together with Dr. Eldon Wilson, they have had a lasting impact on the people receiving ministry. For us as pastors, these special gatherings were the highlights of the year: church members, confirmation/identification of their calling and place in the local church, insights about past, present and future, specific instructions, sometimes corrections or warnings in love. These members were always encouraged and further equipped for the work of the ministry as they received tools to "wage the good warfare, having faith and a good conscience."

For quite some years we have been the Fedele's contacts for the Netherlands, taking care of their ministry schedule. Practically every church in which they minister wants them back and we wholeheartedly recommend them. We pray the Lord will continue to use them in an increasingly effective way for many, many years to come!"

Henk & Corrie Karelse, Pastor Emeritus, "De Banier", Almelo, Netherland

A Word from Machiel and Yvonne Jonker, Pastor AG Sjaloom Church, Heerhugowaard, Netherlands, General Superintendent, Dutch AG.

We have the privilege of knowing the Fedeles for approximately 8 years. Their wonderful Prophetic Voice International Ministry has restored our faith in the Prophetic Office. Both the teaching about the prophetic, as well as the abundance of prophetic words we have heard from them, have blessed us and given testimony of the authenticity of this ministry. For sure Brother Steve and Sister Rita Fedele are prophets of the Lord. In our family life as well as in the church, we have seen the prophetic word spoken and doors opened. Uncountable stories can be told about the fruits of the ministry.

A word of prophecy that stands out was given to a brother in his fifties, unmarried. The word was that he would become a father of many sons! A few years later, Europe was flooded by many refugees from the Middle East. One of them was a young man from Iraq. He came to the Lord and soon after led another young Muslim from Afghanistan to Jesus. Because they were without a home Baba Ate (the man who received the word) took pity on them and offered them shelter. Ate is a Dutch name, but Baba is the Farsi name for father. This released a small revival and in a period of 5 years, approximately a hundred young Muslim men and a few women from

Afghanistan came to the Lord. Some of them, up to 12 at a time, were living in the house of Baba Ate. This man in his fifties became a father for all these converted young Muslims! Just amazing! The prophetic word became flesh.

As a leader, I have admired the attitude of the Fedeles, always submitting to the local leadership. They demonstrate sharp insight not only from a prophetic point of view but also with an apostolic anointing and a shepherd's heart. They have a sharp insight into many church issues and when asked, offered us good council. This gave me all the freedom of heart to introduce them in several Dutch assemblies of God churches, some of which had no history of prophets in the house. All the pastors, without exception, gave a good report.

Special for us were the times in Romania. The Romanian church culture is abundant in prophecy but in general, lacked insight into the proper protocol. The inviting pastors were released and blessed to hear the high teaching levels regarding the prophetic. In our local church, we are honored that the Fedeles are willing to bestow advice in the apostolic office.

An extra word of appreciation for all the years of living in suitcases and pouring out their lives in the service of the Lord. Holland is blessed by this great ministry, serving the church and serving our nation.

A Word from Hans & Esther Tims

National Leaders Friends for Ministries in Fellowship (FMF)

It's all about Jesus, uplifting the body of Christ, building the church and expanding the Kingdom of God to function in His perfect will. Their apostolic and prophetic teaching gives courage, confirmation, and direction. Steve and Rita Fedele helped us enormously in building the church. Their ministry, teachings, sermons and prophetic words for ourselves, our leadership, and church members have been priceless.

Even now in our season of leading leaders in the Netherlands throughout our network, Friends for Ministries in Fellowship, the Fedeles stand with us and have a great impact and influence for our Nation.

A Word from Marcus Gunner

In May 2015 my wife and I visited a meeting that took place in a friend's church in the Netherlands. Stephen and Rita, whom I saw for the first time, ministered that night. During the ministry time I found myself translating a prophecy for my parents who are the senior leaders of our home church when suddenly Rita and then Stephen directly addressed me. Besides speaking about personal involvement in ministry, they spoke about a season of two and a half years that would come to an end. A season in which the enemy tried to destroy the call of God on my life by putting me in a place of feeling useless and dishonored, and in which he tried to let me feel like I brought embarrassment and shame. But now the Lord would bring newness to my life.

In this context, I need to mention that my wife and I had been married for about four and a half years back then. While my siblings and close friends would have babies, my wife would not get pregnant. After ongoing circles of hope and disappointment we decided to go to doctors who confirmed that due to my physical situation, it would be like winning the lottery if we had a natural pregnancy. Being aware of the many miracles in that area that God's word is speaking about, we came to a state of hope that was again and again interrupted by a certain degree of hopelessness and resignation in order to protect ourselves from the next moment of grief and despair. About three years after my wife and I started trying to become pregnant and only a couple months after we got to know Stephen and Rita, we found out how precise these words of God were and how they were pointing to a moment that would become a huge blessing for us and a remarkable testimony to our environment and especially to many in the streets of Israel.

We had just returned from our second street music trip in October 2015 - these came into life to bring love and joy to the hearts of individuals on the streets of Israel in these times of growing anti-Semitism and to provide an environment where people can encounter God through music. When we found out that my wife was pregnant, the Story of our God given little Anna and the promise that the God of Abraham, Isaac, and Jacob blesses those who bless Israel and the Jewish people has been shared literally dozens of times in Jerusalem and other Israeli cities. It has evoked many tears, applauses, smiles and deep talks. We really appreciate Stephen and Rita as people who became friends but also especially for their approach in ministry which is characterized by humility and a deep understanding of the church and respect for its God given order within the frame of the five- fold ministry.

A Word from Jean Luc Trachsel, Evangelist and founder
of (AIMG) International Healing Association, Switzerland

Steve and Rita Fedele have been precious friends for many years. We acknowledge and enjoy their prophetic ministry! With a great sensitivity to the Spirit and always submitted to local authorities, they bring support, wisdom and encouragement to ministries and churches. They have been a prophetic voice for important decisions we had to make for our churches, ministry, our business and private life. We highly recommend their ministry that is driven by a spirit of service and humility.

Jean Luc Trachsel, Evangelist

A Word from Pastor Philippe Montuire

I'm a witness to the impact of Steve and Rita's ministry in Europe. Their prophetic ministry and their teachings on the fivefold ministry had a great influence on many people. Today, they work with several apostolic networks in France. When I look back to the first years of their coming, I see God's faithfulness in bringing forth the fruit of their ministry in my country. I also realize how much I'm blessed to know them and to have them as mentors and a spiritual father and mother in the faith.

I met Pastor Steve Fedele at the end of 1994 in Canada. The next summer, he came to France with his wife, Rita, and their children. They ministered to the church I was pastoring at that time and from then on, our relationship has only grown stronger over the years. Since then, every year, I set up the schedule for Steve and Rita's ministry in France, Belgium, and Switzerland. In the first years, Steve often came by himself and I had the privilege to travel with him. These were times where I received and learned so much. I learned watching Steve serving the Lord in every kind of church, small or large, open to the prophetic or skeptical, close or far away. I witnessed the same dedication and the same love for the people of God, night after night, week after week. Steve and Rita stayed faithful, and still are, to visit the churches in Europe and pioneer the message of the five-fold ministry.

The beginnings were humbling and they often spent their health and sometimes their money to be faithful to the call of God and because of their faithfulness, many people and churches have been blessed and established.

Pastor Philippe Montuire

Bibliography

Bible Hub. (2018) Hitchcock's Dictionary of Bible Names. Retrieved from: http://biblehub.com/topical/p/paul.htm

Crouch, Andre. (1972). The Tribute. Lyrics Mode. Retrieved from: http://www.lyricsmode.com

NAMI. (2015). Mental Health by the Numbers. Retrieved from: https://www.nami.org/learn-more/mental-health-by-the-numbers.

Simon, Carly. *I Haven't Got Time for the Pain.*

Storms, Sam. *What Does Scripture Teach About the Office of Prophet and Gift of Prophet?* October 8, 2015. Retrieved from:https://www.thegospelcoalition.org/article/sam-storms-what-does-scripture-teach-about-office-prophet-gift-prophecy/ .

Wiersbe, Dr. Warren W. BE Concordance. Publisher David C. Cook. Taken from: Bible Gateway.

Williams, Matt. *The Prodigal Son's Father Shouldn't Have Run! Putting Luke 15:11-32 in context.* Biola.(Summer, 2010).Retrieved from: http://magazine.biola.edu/article/10-

.

Prophetic Voice Ministries

I pray that this book has been an inspiration and encouragement to you and that you have come to understand God really has a plan and a purpose for your life. You can learn more about our ministry and the way we can serve you by contacting us for prayer, encouragement and prophetic insight. Contact us at:

WWW.PropheticVoiceministriesInternational.com

While on our website make sure to browse the numerous services available, especially through the Prophetic Consultation Service (PCS).

Also, check out our Facebook page. Comments and testimonies are welcome

Much peace and blessings,

Prophet Stephen Fedele

Made in the USA
Middletown, DE
19 October 2021